DRIVEN BY DOPAMINE RULED BY CORTISOL

The Hidden Cycle of
Modern Craving, Stress and Burnout

SUBRATA KUMAR PATEL

This book is intended for informational and educational purposes only. The content reflects the author's perspectives, observations, and interpretations related to human behavior, attention, stress, and modern psychological patterns. It is not intended as medical, psychological, or professional healthcare advice.

The author and publisher disclaim responsibility for any adverse effects resulting directly or indirectly from the use or application of the information contained in this book.

First Edition — 2026

Written by Subrata Kumar Patel

ACKNOWLEDGMENT

This book was shaped not only by research and reflection, but by years of observing people, conversations, workplaces, pressures, ambitions, and the quiet emotional struggles often hidden beneath everyday life.

I would like to express my gratitude to my family, mentors, colleagues, friends and to everyone who, knowingly or unknowingly, contributed to the thoughts explored in these pages. Every interaction, challenge, observation, and moment of reflection helped deepen my understanding of how modern life influences attention, stress, behavior, and emotional balance.

Most importantly, I would like to thank the readers of this book.

Your willingness to pause, reflect, and understand yourself more consciously in a world designed for constant stimulation is deeply meaningful. I hope these pages offer not only insight, but also moments of clarity, awareness, and quiet recognition.

PREFACE

We live in a world that constantly competes for our attention.

Every day, we navigate a growing stream of information, responsibilities, notifications, expectations, and opportunities for engagement. We move quickly between tasks, respond to multiple demands, and remain connected almost all the time. Yet despite having more tools, convenience, and access to information than any generation before us, many people find themselves feeling mentally restless, emotionally fatigued, and increasingly distracted.

This book was written for anyone who has ever felt mentally busy but not fully present, constantly connected but not necessarily fulfilled, or productive on the outside while feeling internally exhausted. These experiences are becoming increasingly common, yet few people stop long enough to understand the forces contributing to them.

The purpose of this book is not to encourage fear of technology, ambition, productivity, or modern life. These are all valuable parts of the world we live in. Instead, the goal is to develop a deeper understanding of how modern environments interact with the mind and how greater awareness can help us respond more intentionally.

As you move through these chapters, you will explore how reward-seeking and stress-response systems influence attention, habits, emotions, and everyday behavior. More importantly, you will discover why awareness plays such an important role in creating meaningful and sustainable change.

I encourage you to read these pages with curiosity rather than judgment. The patterns described throughout this book are not signs of weakness or failure. They are human responses to environments that continuously shape the way we think, feel, and behave.

The more clearly we understand those influences, the more consciously we can choose how to live within them.

And that understanding is where the journey of awareness begins.

Contents

Introduction		**1**
Chapter 1	**The Hidden Chemistry of Modern Life**	**7**
	Section 1: The Modern Overload	9
	Section 2: Why Willpower Fails	15
	Section 3: Introducing Dopamine and Cortisol	19
	Section 4: Why Awareness Changes Everything	24
Chapter 2	**Dopamine — The Brain's Reward Seeker**	**29**
	Section 1: Dopamine and the Pursuit of reward	31
	Section 2: The Habit Loop	36
	Section 3: Digital Dopamine Traps	41
	Section 4: Motivation, Craving and Temporary Relief	46
Chapter 3	**Cortisol: Living Under Constant Pressure**	**51**
	Section 1: The Stress System at Work	53
	Section 2: Burnout, Mental Fatigue and Emotional Exhaustion	58
	Section 3: When Stress Becomes Your Normal State	63
Chapter 4	**The Dopamine–Cortisol Cycle**	**69**
	Section 1: How Stress Fuels Stimulation	71

	Section 2: The Cycle in Everyday Life	77
	Section 3: Breaking the Reward–Stress Pattern	82
Chapter 5	**From Reactivity to Awareness**	**87**
	Section 1: The Awareness Gap	89
	Section 2: Recognizing Your Internal Patterns	95
	Section 3: The Power of Conscious Attention	100
Chapter 6	**Mastering Your Internal Systems**	**105**
	Section 1: Regulating Dopamine - Rebalancing the Pull	107
	Section 2: Calming Cortisol — Restoring Stability	112
	Section 3: Rebuilding Attention and Mental Clarity	117
	Section 4: Creating Internal Balance Through Awareness	122
Chapter 7	**The Modern Environment: Designed to Capture You**	**127**
	Section 1: The Attention Economy	129
	Section 2: How Digital Environments Shape Behavior	134
	Section 3: Creating Space Within a Distracted World	139
Chapter 8	**Living With Awareness in a Distracted World**	**145**
	Section 1: Awareness in Everyday Life	147
	Section 2: Building Sustainable Mental Habits	152

Section 3: The Daily Control Framework 157
Section 4: Long-Term Change Through Small Shifts 163
Conclusion Returning to Yourself 168

Final Reflections 173
About the Author 175

INTRODUCTION

Driven by Dopamine, Ruled by Cortisol

For a long time, I believed the constant mental exhaustion I experienced was simply part of modern life.

Like many people, I stayed busy, productive, connected, and constantly engaged. My days were filled with responsibilities, conversations, deadlines, notifications, decisions, and endless streams of information competing for attention. From the outside, everything appeared normal. Work continued. Life moved forward. Goals were pursued. Tasks were completed.

But internally, something felt increasingly unsettled.

Even during moments meant for rest, my mind rarely felt fully quiet. I would sit down after a long day intending to relax for a few minutes, only to find myself automatically reaching for my phone, checking notifications, scrolling through content, switching between videos, messages, articles, and unfinished thoughts without any clear intention. Hours could disappear inside small fragments of stimulation that never truly felt satisfying, yet somehow kept my attention engaged.

What disturbed me most was not the behavior itself.

It was how normal it had become.

Over time, I began noticing the same patterns everywhere around me. People were constantly connected, yet mentally exhausted. Attention spans seemed increasingly fragmented. Silence felt uncomfortable. Rest no longer felt deeply restorative. Even moments of pause were quickly filled with stimulation. Many of us had become accustomed to living in a continuous state of mental engagement without fully recognizing its effects.

The more I observed these patterns, both within myself and in the modern environments around me, the more I realized that something deeper was happening beneath the surface of everyday behavior.

This was not simply about discipline.

It was not laziness, weakness, or lack of motivation.

Many of the struggles people experience today are deeply connected to invisible internal systems constantly shaping attention, behavior, emotional reactions, stress responses, and the pursuit of relief.

Two of the most powerful systems involved in this process are dopamine and cortisol.

Dopamine drives anticipation, seeking, craving, and the pursuit of reward. It pushes attention toward what feels stimulating, engaging, or potentially satisfying. Cortisol, on the other hand, responds to pressure, uncertainty, tension, and stress. It prepares the mind and body to stay alert, reactive, and ready to respond.

Individually, both systems are necessary.

But within modern environments built around constant stimulation, endless information, digital engagement, pressure, urgency, and emotional overload, these systems often begin interacting in ways that quietly shape everyday behavior far more than most people realize.

Stress increases the desire for relief. Relief often arrives through stimulation.

The stimulation provides temporary escape, distraction, or reward.

But the relief fades quickly, and the cycle quietly begins again.

Over time, this creates patterns that influence how we focus, rest, react, consume information, handle discomfort, and experience everyday life itself.

What makes these patterns especially powerful is that they often operate automatically. Many reactions happen so quickly and so repeatedly that they stop feeling like reactions at all. They begin to feel normal. Sometimes they even begin to feel like personalities.

That realization changed the way I understood modern life.

I began seeing that many people are not simply struggling with distraction. They are living inside environments carefully designed to compete for attention while continuously interacting with biological systems that evolved for survival, reward, and adaptation. The result is a state of constant mental movement that slowly fragments attention, increases emotional fatigue, and weakens our ability to remain fully present and intentional.

Yet the purpose of this book is not to create fear around technology, ambition, productivity, or modern life itself.

Nor is it about becoming perfectly disciplined or completely disconnected from the world.

The goal is much simpler — and much more important.

It is to develop awareness.

Because awareness changes the relationship we have with our patterns.

The moment you begin noticing how stress influences behavior, how stimulation shapes attention, and how automatic reactions quietly repeat themselves throughout daily life, something begins to shift. You may still feel the impulse, distraction, pressure, or craving, but you are no longer completely unconscious inside the cycle.

That awareness creates space.

And within that space, choice slowly becomes possible again.

This book is an exploration of those invisible patterns — how they shape modern behavior, why they feel increasingly difficult to escape, and how greater awareness can help us regain clarity, attention, emotional balance, and a more intentional relationship with ourselves.

Because in many ways, modern life is no longer driven only by external demands.

It is increasingly shaped by internal cycles we rarely stop long enough to fully see.

CHAPTER 1

THE HIDDEN CHEMISTRY OF MODERN LIFE

SECTION 1: THE MODERN OVERLOAD

You don't notice it happening at first.

Most days begin quietly and automatically. Before your mind has fully settled into the morning, something is already pulling at your attention — a message waiting to be checked, unfinished tasks from the previous day, notifications, reminders, updates, conversations, and thoughts competing for space almost immediately after waking up. The day begins before you have fully arrived inside it.

And over time, this starts to feel normal.

You move through the day responding continuously. Messages are answered, tasks are switched, information is consumed, and attention moves rapidly between different demands. Even moments that appear calm on the surface rarely feel mentally quiet underneath. The mind remains active, anticipating what comes next, thinking about what still needs attention, or searching for something else to engage with.

You are not just living your day.

You are responding to it.

What makes this difficult to recognize is how ordinary the pattern feels. Constant mental movement has become deeply integrated into modern life. Attention shifts so frequently that uninterrupted focus begins to feel unusual. Even brief moments of pause are quickly filled. Waiting becomes scrolling. Silence becomes stimulation. Rest becomes another form of engagement.

The mind rarely experiences complete stillness anymore.

At first, this may not seem harmful. The behavior feels productive, connected, and efficient. But over time, something deeper begins to change. The mind becomes increasingly accustomed to constant input, and as that happens, sustained attention becomes more difficult to maintain. Small interruptions begin carrying more power. Stillness feels unfamiliar. And activities that require depth, patience, or uninterrupted focus begin to feel mentally heavier than they once did.

Alongside this constant stimulation, there is another force operating quietly beneath the surface — pressure.

Modern life does not simply demand attention. It also creates continuous psychological tension. Responsibilities remain unfinished, expectations continue expanding, and the feeling that something still requires attention rarely disappears completely. Even during periods of rest, part of the mind often remains attached to what is pending, unresolved, or approaching next.

Nothing urgent may be happening in the moment.

Yet the system rarely feels fully at ease.

This creates one of the defining conditions of modern life: a state where stimulation and pressure operate together continuously. You are pulled toward engagement while simultaneously pushed by responsibility, urgency, comparison, and mental overload. Attention becomes fragmented not only because the environment is distracting, but because the mind itself remains in a constant state of movement.

Over time, this repeated activation begins to feel like your natural baseline. A busy mind feels familiar. Restlessness feels ordinary. Continuous mental engagement starts feeling normal simply because it has been repeated so often.

But familiarity is not the same as balance.

Most people attempt to solve this experience at the surface level. They try to become more disciplined, more productive, more efficient, or more organized. They reduce distractions temporarily, create stricter routines, and push themselves toward greater control. These efforts may help for short periods, but they often fail to create lasting change because they address behavior without fully understanding what is driving it.

The deeper issue is not simply what you are doing.

It is what your system is continuously responding to beneath awareness.

Behind your thoughts, actions, habits, and emotional reactions, there are internal systems constantly interpreting stimulation, pressure, uncertainty, reward, and tension. These systems shape attention and behavior long before conscious thought fully enters the process.

You do not experience only the world around you.

You experience how your internal system reacts to it.

Once you begin observing closely, certain patterns become difficult to ignore. Attention shifts more easily than expected. Small interruptions quickly pull focus away. The mind searches for novelty even when there is no real need for it. At the same time, relatively small demands can create disproportionate mental tension.

This is not random inconsistency.

It is patterned conditioning.

The modern environment continuously trains the mind toward stimulation, responsiveness, anticipation, and alertness. And when a system remains activated for too long, it does not become calmer, clearer, or more balanced.

It becomes reactive.

Understanding this is where awareness begins.

Not through immediate control or forced discipline, but through recognizing what is happening beneath the surface of everyday life. Because when you begin seeing the forces shaping your attention, your behavior, and your internal state more clearly, you also begin creating distance from them.

And within that distance, a different way of living slowly becomes possible.

Key Insights

- Modern life keeps attention in a state of continuous response.
- Constant stimulation gradually reduces mental stillness and depth of focus.
- Pressure and stimulation often operate together beneath awareness.
- What feels normal may actually be a conditioned state of reactivity.

- Awareness begins by recognizing the patterns shaping your attention and behavior.

SECTION 2: WHY WILLPOWER FAILS

Most people already know many of the habits that negatively affect their attention, focus, sleep, and emotional balance.

They know excessive scrolling leaves them mentally drained. They know constant distraction weakens concentration. They know staying connected all the time increases stress and mental fatigue. Yet despite understanding these patterns intellectually, many people still find themselves repeating the same behaviors every day.

This often creates frustration.

You decide to focus more seriously, reduce distractions, sleep earlier, spend less time on your phone, or become more disciplined. For a short time, the effort works. Motivation feels strong. Attention improves. You feel more in control.

But eventually, the old patterns quietly return.

A few minutes of distraction becomes an hour. One break becomes repeated interruptions. The phone is checked automatically without any clear reason. Focus weakens again, not because you stopped caring, but because the behavior itself operates more automatically than most people realize.

This is where many people begin blaming themselves.

They assume the problem is laziness, lack of discipline, weak motivation, or poor self-control. But the reality is often far more complex. Human behavior is not shaped by willpower alone. Much of what people do repeatedly is influenced by patterns that operate beneath conscious awareness.

The mind naturally moves toward what feels immediately relieving, stimulating, familiar, or rewarding — especially during moments of stress, boredom, discomfort, uncertainty, or mental fatigue.

This is why willpower often feels inconsistent.

You may genuinely want to focus, yet still feel pulled toward distraction. You may want rest, yet continue scrolling late into the night. You may recognize that something is draining your energy while simultaneously struggling to stop repeating it.

These contradictions confuse many people because they assume conscious intention should automatically control behavior.

But behavior is rarely driven only by intention.

Much of modern life continuously conditions attention toward immediacy, stimulation, responsiveness, and relief. Over time, the brain begins adapting to those repeated patterns. Small urges become automatic reactions. Temporary distractions become deeply reinforced habits. And because these behaviors are repeated so frequently, they eventually begin feeling natural.

This is why many people experience a cycle of temporary control followed by repeated relapse into old patterns. The issue is not simply a lack of discipline. The deeper issue is that the environment, the nervous system, emotional discomfort, and repeated behavioral conditioning are often working together more powerfully than willpower alone.

Willpower can create short-term resistance. But awareness creates understanding.

And understanding changes the way you respond to yourself.

Instead of constantly fighting behavior through guilt, pressure, or self-criticism, you begin recognizing the deeper patterns influencing your reactions in the first place. You begin noticing when attention is searching for relief, when discomfort triggers distraction, and when habits are operating automatically beneath conscious thought.

That awareness does not instantly eliminate the behavior.

But it changes your relationship with it.

Because the moment you clearly recognize a pattern while it is happening, you are no longer completely controlled by it.

Key Insights

- Willpower fades when patterns remain unchanged.
- Many behaviors feel automatic because they have been repeated for too long.
- Lasting change begins with understanding what is driving your reactions.

SECTION 3: INTRODUCING DOPAMINE AND CORTISOL

To understand why modern life feels increasingly difficult to slow down from, it is important to understand two systems that quietly influence much of human behavior: dopamine and cortisol.

Most people have heard these terms before, often in simplified ways. Dopamine is usually described as the "feel-good chemical," while cortisol is commonly called the "stress hormone." But their actual roles are far more complex — and far more connected to everyday life than many people realize.

Dopamine is not simply about pleasure.

It is deeply connected to anticipation, motivation, seeking, and the pursuit of reward. It activates when the brain expects something potentially rewarding or stimulating. This is why the desire to check a notification can sometimes feel stronger than the satisfaction of actually seeing it. The system becomes driven not only by reward itself, but by the possibility of reward.

This pattern appears constantly in modern life.

You check your phone quickly while working, not because something important definitely happened, but because something might have happened. You continue scrolling even after losing interest because the mind keeps expecting the next piece of content to feel more engaging than the last. The anticipation itself keeps attention moving forward.

Over time, the brain becomes increasingly responsive to novelty, stimulation, and unpredictability.

Cortisol operates differently.

Its primary role is to help the body respond to pressure, uncertainty, challenge, and potential threat. In healthy situations, cortisol is useful. It increases alertness, sharpens attention temporarily, and helps the body prepare for action when something important requires energy or focus.

But modern stress rarely arrives in short, isolated moments.

Instead, many people experience low but continuous psychological pressure throughout the day. Unfinished tasks, constant availability, financial concerns, social comparison, deadlines, digital overload, and mental overstimulation keep the system activated far longer than it was originally designed for.

As a result, many people no longer move cleanly between stress and recovery.

The mind remains partially alert even during rest.

This is where dopamine and cortisol begin interacting in ways that quietly shape everyday behavior.

Stress creates discomfort, tension, or mental fatigue. The mind naturally begins searching for relief. Dopamine-driven behaviors — scrolling, checking notifications, consuming content, switching tasks, or seeking stimulation — often provide temporary escape from that discomfort.

But the relief is usually short-lived.

Once the stimulation fades, the underlying tension often returns, which creates the urge to seek relief again. Over time, this can create repetitive cycles where stress increases the desire for stimulation, and stimulation temporarily reduces awareness of stress without truly resolving it.

Most people experience this pattern without fully recognizing it.

You may feel mentally exhausted yet still continue consuming stimulation late into the night. You may struggle to focus on important work while repeatedly checking distractions that provide only temporary relief. You may want genuine rest, yet feel uncomfortable sitting quietly without engaging with something.

These reactions are not random.

They are deeply connected to how modern environments continuously interact with the brain's reward and stress systems.

Understanding this changes something important.

Many behaviors that people blame entirely on lack of discipline begin making more sense when viewed through the interaction between stimulation, stress, anticipation, discomfort, and relief. The goal is not to remove dopamine or eliminate stress completely. Both systems are necessary parts of being human.

The real shift begins when you become aware of how these systems are influencing your attention, reactions, habits, and emotional patterns throughout daily life.

Because once you begin recognizing the cycle clearly, you stop seeing your behavior as random weakness.

You begin seeing the system underneath it.

Key Insights

- Dopamine drives anticipation, seeking, and the pursuit of stimulation.

- Cortisol keeps the mind and body alert during stress and pressure.
- Modern life continuously activates both reward and stress systems together.
- Many distracting behaviors are attempts to relieve discomfort temporarily.
- Awareness begins by recognizing the patterns operating beneath automatic behavior.

SECTION 4: WHY AWARENESS CHANGES EVERYTHING

Most people try to change their behavior by fighting the behavior directly.

They force stricter routines, set stronger goals, remove distractions temporarily, or push themselves toward greater discipline. Sometimes these efforts work for a short period. Motivation increases, focus improves, and the feeling of control briefly returns.

But many people eventually find themselves falling back into the same patterns again.

Not because they do not care.

Not because they are incapable of change.

But because lasting change rarely begins with force alone.

It begins with awareness.

Awareness changes something fundamental about the way you experience your own behavior. The moment you begin noticing your reactions while they are happening, the pattern no longer operates completely unconsciously.

You start recognizing the moments that previously happened automatically.

You notice the urge to check your phone the moment discomfort appears during focused work. You notice how quickly boredom creates the impulse to search for stimulation. You begin recognizing how stress quietly influences attention, mood, emotional reactions, and decision-making throughout the day.

These moments may seem small.

But they change the relationship you have with yourself.

Before awareness, many behaviors feel immediate and unquestioned. The reaction happens so quickly that there is little space between impulse and action. Attention moves automatically toward whatever feels most relieving, stimulating, or emotionally comforting in the moment.

Awareness interrupts that automatic movement.

For the first time, you begin observing the pattern instead of being completely absorbed inside it.

That observation creates distance.

And within that distance, choice slowly becomes possible again.

This is why awareness matters more deeply than many people realize. Awareness is not passive observation. It is the beginning of understanding how your internal system actually responds to pressure, stimulation, uncertainty, discomfort, and reward.

Without awareness, people often remain trapped in cycles they cannot clearly see. They continue blaming themselves while repeating patterns that have already become deeply conditioned beneath conscious thought.

But once the pattern becomes visible, something begins to shift internally.

You stop viewing yourself only through the behavior.

You begin recognizing the systems influencing the behavior.

That does not mean change becomes immediate or effortless. The impulses may still appear. Distractions may still feel tempting. Stress may still trigger old reactions. But awareness reduces automatic participation in the cycle.

And over time, that changes everything.

Because real change is rarely created through self-criticism, guilt, or constant internal pressure.

Sustainable change begins when you develop the ability to recognize what is happening inside you clearly enough to respond consciously instead of reacting automatically.

This is where attention slowly becomes more intentional.

This is where emotional patterns become easier to understand.

And this is where the possibility of balance begins to return.

Key Insights

- Awareness creates space between impulse and reaction.
- Many behaviors lose power once they become visible.
- Real change begins with understanding patterns, not fighting yourself constantly.
- You cannot consciously change patterns you do not recognize.
- Awareness turns automatic reactions into conscious choices over time.

CHAPTER 2

DOPAMINE — THE BRAIN'S REWARD SEEKER

SECTION 1: DOPAMINE AND THE PURSUIT OF REWARD

Most people think dopamine is simply the chemical responsible for pleasure or happiness.

But dopamine is less about enjoyment itself and more about anticipation — the feeling of wanting, seeking, expecting, and moving toward something that might feel rewarding. It plays a major role in motivation, curiosity, learning, and attention. Without dopamine, human beings would struggle to pursue goals, stay motivated, or remain engaged with life.

The problem is not dopamine itself.

The problem is the environment constantly competing for it.

Modern life is filled with systems specifically designed to capture attention by triggering anticipation repeatedly. Notifications, short-form videos, social media feeds, recommendations, headlines, messages, and endless streams of new content continuously encourage the brain to keep searching for the next rewarding moment.

And the search itself becomes powerful.

You may open your phone for one specific reason, then continue moving from one app to another without fully intending to. You may scroll long after the experience stops feeling genuinely enjoyable. You may refresh notifications repeatedly even when nothing important is happening. In many cases, the anticipation of something interesting becomes stronger than the actual satisfaction you receive from it.

This is how dopamine quietly shapes attention.

The brain begins learning that stimulation could appear at any moment. A message, a like, a video, a recommendation, or some new piece of information may provide a small emotional reward, and because the reward is unpredictable, attention keeps returning in search of the next one.

Over time, this repeated cycle begins changing the way many people engage with everyday life.

Activities that provide slower or deeper rewards — reading carefully, thinking patiently, working with sustained focus, sitting quietly, or engaging fully with one task — may begin feeling less stimulating by comparison. The mind gradually becomes more accustomed to speed, novelty, and constant engagement.

This does not happen because people become weak.

It happens because the brain adapts to repeated patterns of stimulation.

One of the clearest signs of this shift is the growing difficulty many people experience with boredom. Moments that once felt neutral now quickly trigger the urge to check something, consume something, or move attention elsewhere. The mind becomes increasingly uncomfortable with inactivity because it has been repeatedly conditioned toward stimulation.

This is why dopamine-driven behavior often feels automatic.

The action itself may appear small — checking a phone briefly, opening another tab, refreshing a feed — but the pattern underneath is much deeper. The brain is not simply reacting to content. It is reacting to anticipation, novelty, and the possibility of reward.

And because modern environments provide those possibilities continuously, the cycle rarely fully stops on its own.

Understanding this changes the way many behaviors begin to make sense.

What people often describe as lack of focus, low discipline, or poor attention is sometimes the result of a system that has become overstimulated by constant novelty and repeated reward-seeking behavior. The mind becomes trained to expect continuous engagement, making stillness, patience, and sustained concentration feel increasingly difficult.

But awareness changes the relationship with the pattern.

The moment you begin noticing how often your attention moves automatically toward stimulation, you start recognizing the system underneath the behavior. You begin seeing that many impulses are not random decisions happening consciously in the moment, but conditioned reactions shaped through repetition over time.

And once the pattern becomes visible, attention slowly becomes easier to understand — and eventually, easier to guide more intentionally.

Key Insights

- Dopamine is driven more by anticipation than by pleasure itself.

- Modern digital environments continuously compete for attention through reward-seeking behavior.
- Repeated stimulation gradually conditions the brain toward novelty and interruption.
- Many distracting behaviors are automatic patterns, not conscious decisions.
- Awareness begins by recognizing how attention is repeatedly pulled toward stimulation.

SECTION 2: THE HABIT LOOP

Many behaviors begin as conscious choices.

But repetition slowly changes them into patterns that operate with very little awareness.

At first, checking your phone may feel intentional. You respond to a message, search for information, or take a short break from work. The action appears small and harmless. But when the same behavior is repeated frequently — especially during moments of boredom, stress, uncertainty, or mental fatigue — the brain begins linking certain emotional states with certain responses.

Over time, the pattern becomes automatic.

A moment of discomfort appears, and attention immediately searches for relief. A task becomes mentally demanding, and the urge to check something appears almost instantly. Silence creates restlessness. Waiting triggers scrolling. The reaction often happens so quickly that people notice the behavior only after they are already inside it.

This is how habit loops quietly form.

Most loops follow a similar structure:

A trigger creates discomfort, anticipation, boredom, stress, or emotional tension. The brain then moves toward a behavior associated with stimulation or relief. For a short time, the behavior reduces discomfort or creates a small reward. The brain remembers that temporary relief, making the pattern easier to repeat the next time a similar feeling appears.

The more often this cycle repeats, the more automatic it becomes.

This is why many people continue behaviors even when they no longer feel deeply satisfying. The reward itself is often brief, but the brain remembers the possibility of relief, stimulation, or escape connected to the action.

Modern digital environments strengthen these loops continuously.

Short-form videos, endless scrolling, autoplay systems, notifications, recommendations, and rapid content switching all encourage repeated behavioral cycles built around anticipation and instant engagement. The brain rarely receives a natural stopping point. One piece of stimulation immediately leads to another.

And because the rewards are unpredictable, the pattern becomes even more powerful.

Sometimes the content feels interesting. Sometimes it does not. But the uncertainty itself keeps attention engaged because the brain continues expecting that the next moment might feel more rewarding than the previous one.

This is why people often lose track of time while scrolling or switching between apps. The behavior stops being fully intentional and starts becoming reactive. Attention keeps moving automatically toward stimulation because the loop has already been reinforced many times before.

Over time, these repeated cycles influence more than just screen habits.

Patience becomes weaker. Deep focus feels harder to maintain. Small discomforts become more difficult to tolerate without distraction. The mind becomes increasingly trained to escape interruption, boredom, uncertainty, or emotional tension quickly instead of remaining present with the experience.

This is important to understand because many people judge themselves harshly for behaviors that have already become deeply conditioned patterns.

But conditioned patterns are not broken through guilt alone.

They first need to be recognized clearly.

The moment you begin noticing your triggers, your automatic reactions, and the emotional states driving certain behaviors, the habit loop becomes easier to understand. And when a pattern becomes visible, it slowly becomes possible to interrupt it before the cycle completes itself automatically.

That is where awareness begins changing behavior.

Not by forcing perfection. But by helping you recognize the loop while it is happening.

Key Insights

- Habits become automatic through repeated emotional and behavioral patterns.
- Many distractions are responses to discomfort, boredom, stress, or mental fatigue.
- Digital environments continuously reinforce fast reward-seeking loops.
- Repeated stimulation weakens patience and sustained focus over time.
- Awareness begins by recognizing the triggers and patterns behind automatic behavior.

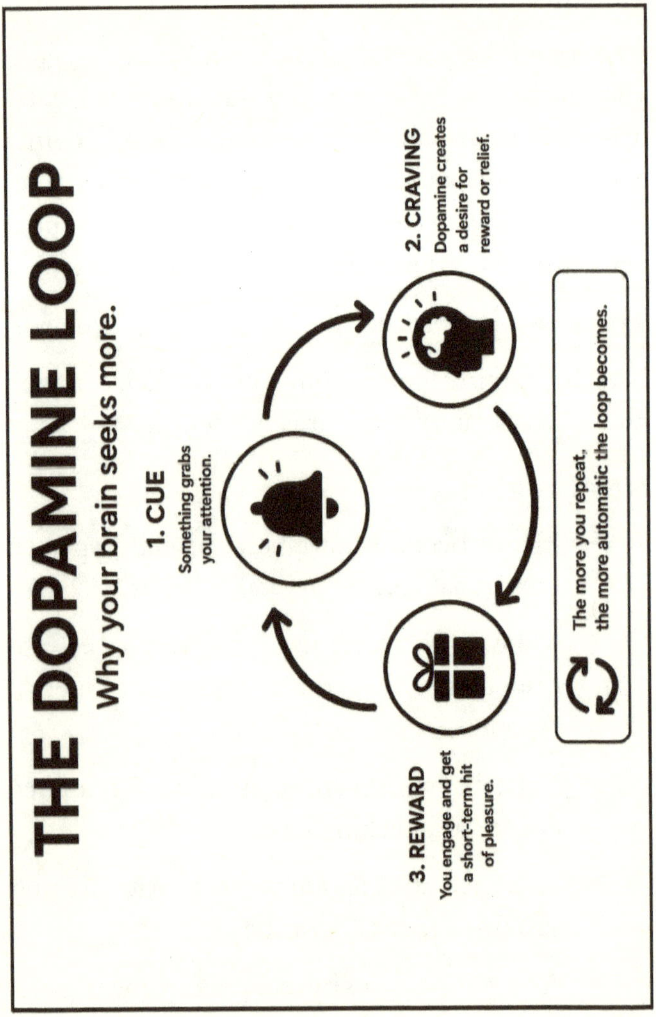
THE DOPAMINE LOOP
Why your brain seeks more.
1. CUE
Something grabs your attention.
2. CRAVING
Dopamine creates a desire for reward or relief.
3. REWARD
You engage and get a short-term hit of pleasure.
The more you repeat, the more automatic the loop becomes.

SECTION 3: DIGITAL DOPAMINE TRAPS

Digital technology is not harmful simply because it exists.

The challenge is that many modern digital systems are intentionally designed to keep attention engaged for as long as possible. Their success often depends on how effectively they can hold focus, encourage repeated interaction, and continuously stimulate anticipation.

This is where dopamine becomes deeply involved.

Most digital platforms operate through small but repeated reward patterns. Notifications appear unpredictably. Content refreshes endlessly. Recommendations adapt constantly. New information, entertainment, validation, or stimulation always seem available just one more click, scroll, or refresh away.

The brain quickly learns to expect these possibilities.

And because the rewards are inconsistent and unpredictable, attention becomes even more attached to the process. Sometimes a notification feels important. Sometimes it does not. Sometimes the next video feels entertaining. Sometimes it feels empty. But uncertainty itself keeps the system engaged because the mind continues expecting that something more interesting may appear next.

This is why many digital behaviors feel difficult to stop at the right moment.

You may open one video and continue watching several more without planning to. You may check your phone briefly and suddenly realize much more time has passed than expected. You may continue refreshing, scrolling, or browsing even after the experience stops feeling genuinely enjoyable.

The behavior often continues not because satisfaction is increasing, but because anticipation continues.

Over time, this repeated stimulation begins influencing attention itself.

The mind becomes increasingly adapted to speed, novelty, interruption, and rapid emotional shifts. As a result, slower experiences — reading carefully, thinking deeply, staying with one task, or remaining present without stimulation — may begin feeling less engaging by comparison.

This is one reason many people now struggle with sustained focus even when they genuinely want to concentrate.

But digital dopamine traps are not limited to entertainment alone.

The same patterns appear in productivity, work culture, and everyday communication. Constantly checking emails, refreshing messages, monitoring updates, tracking responses, and remaining continuously available can also create repeated cycles of anticipation and reward. The brain begins learning that stimulation, information, or validation could arrive at any moment.

Over time, attention stops resting fully.

It remains partially alert, waiting for the next interruption.

One of the most difficult parts of these patterns is that they often feel productive or socially normal. People may believe they are staying informed, connected, responsive, or efficient while quietly becoming conditioned to continuous engagement.

The issue is not technology itself.

The deeper issue is unconscious overexposure to stimulation without enough awareness, recovery, stillness, or intentional control over attention.

Without awareness, the mind gradually loses the ability to distinguish between meaningful engagement and compulsive engagement. Attention keeps moving automatically toward whatever feels immediately stimulating, emotionally relieving, or temporarily rewarding.

And because modern digital environments are designed to encourage exactly that behavior, the cycle can continue for years without being fully recognized.

Awareness changes that.

The moment you begin noticing how often attention moves automatically toward stimulation, digital habits become easier to observe clearly. You start recognizing when engagement is intentional and when it is simply reactive conditioning repeating itself automatically.

That recognition is important because attention is one of the most valuable resources you possess.

And what repeatedly captures your attention slowly shapes the way you experience your life.

Key Insights

- Many digital platforms are designed to keep attention continuously engaged.
- Unpredictable rewards make digital behaviors especially difficult to stop.
- Repeated stimulation gradually conditions the brain toward speed and novelty.

- Digital dopamine traps also appear in work culture and constant responsiveness.
- Awareness helps distinguish intentional engagement from automatic behavior.

SECTION 4: MOTIVATION, CRAVING AND TEMPORARY RELIEF

Many people assume motivation is a stable force that appears when the mind is ready to focus, work, or change.

But motivation is often far more dependent on emotional state than people realize.

When the mind feels stimulated, inspired, rewarded, or emotionally engaged, motivation can feel strong and natural. Attention moves easily toward goals, productivity increases, and effort feels manageable. But when stress, boredom, fatigue, uncertainty, or emotional discomfort increase, motivation often begins weakening quickly.

This is where craving and temporary relief begin influencing behavior.

Craving is not always intense or dramatic. In everyday life, it often appears as small urges that quietly pull attention toward stimulation, distraction, comfort, or emotional escape. The urge to check something during difficult work. The desire to avoid silence through entertainment. The impulse to seek quick relief during stress or mental fatigue.

These moments happen constantly.

And most of the time, they happen automatically.

The brain naturally prefers experiences that reduce discomfort quickly. If a certain behavior repeatedly provides temporary relief — even for a few moments — the mind begins remembering that association. Over time, the urge itself can become stronger whenever similar emotional states appear again.

This is why many people move toward stimulation most strongly when they feel emotionally drained, stressed, lonely, bored, overwhelmed, or mentally exhausted.

The behavior may look different for different people.

For some, it becomes endless scrolling or binge watching. For others, it becomes constant busyness, emotional eating, compulsive shopping, excessive work, repeated checking behaviors, or continuous entertainment. Sometimes people seek validation, achievement, productivity, or external success not only because they genuinely want those things, but because the pursuit itself temporarily distracts them from discomfort underneath.

The pattern changes form.

But the psychological movement often remains similar:

moving away from discomfort and toward temporary emotional relief.

This is important to understand because many people mistakenly believe that motivation disappears because they are weak, lazy, or incapable of discipline. In reality, the nervous system is often responding to stress, emotional exhaustion, overstimulation, or conditioned reward patterns operating beneath awareness.

Temporary relief is not the same as genuine recovery.

A person may spend hours consuming stimulation and still feel mentally unsettled afterward. Someone may remain constantly busy yet continue feeling emotionally exhausted underneath. The activity creates short-term escape, but not necessarily restoration.

Over time, this can create cycles where people continuously chase stimulation, achievement, distraction, or relief without fully understanding what they are actually trying to escape from internally.

This is why awareness matters so deeply.

The moment you begin recognizing the emotional states driving certain cravings, behaviors become easier to understand. You start noticing when the mind is genuinely choosing something intentionally and when it is simply reacting automatically in search of relief.

That awareness creates an important shift.

Instead of fighting yourself constantly, you begin understanding yourself more clearly.

And understanding changes the way you respond.

Because lasting balance does not come from eliminating every craving or forcing perfect discipline. It begins by recognizing how stress, emotion, reward, and temporary relief quietly shape behavior throughout everyday life.

Key Insights

- Motivation is strongly influenced by emotional and mental state.
- Cravings often appear as automatic attempts to reduce discomfort or seek relief.
- Temporary stimulation may distract the mind without creating genuine recovery.
- Reward-seeking behaviors can take many forms beyond digital distraction.
- Awareness helps reveal the emotional patterns driving automatic behavior.

CHAPTER 3

CORTISOL: LIVING UNDER CONSTANT PRESSURE

SECTION 1: THE STRESS SYSTEM AT WORK

Stress is often misunderstood as something that appears only during major problems, emergencies, or highly difficult situations.

But for many people, stress no longer arrives in isolated moments.

It becomes continuous.

Modern life keeps the mind in a near-constant state of psychological engagement. Responsibilities remain unfinished, expectations continue expanding, decisions never fully stop, and attention is repeatedly pulled in multiple directions throughout the day. Even when nothing immediately dangerous is happening, the nervous system often continues behaving as though something still requires attention.

This is where cortisol plays an important role.

Cortisol is part of the body's natural stress-response system. In healthy situations, it helps increase alertness, energy, and focus when action is necessary. If you face danger, pressure, uncertainty, or an important challenge, cortisol helps prepare the body to respond effectively.

The problem is not cortisol itself.

The problem is prolonged activation without enough recovery.

Human beings were not designed to remain mentally alert every waking hour. Yet many modern environments continuously encourage exactly that state. Emails continue after work hours. Notifications create repeated interruptions. Unfinished responsibilities remain mentally active in the background. Even periods meant for rest are often filled with stimulation, information, or emotional engagement.

As a result, many people no longer experience a clear boundary between stress and recovery.

The body may slow down physically, but the mind often continues carrying pressure internally.

This pattern is especially visible in professional life. Many people function efficiently on the surface while quietly carrying continuous mental tension underneath. Meetings are attended, deadlines are completed, conversations continue normally, and responsibilities are managed successfully. Yet genuine psychological recovery becomes increasingly rare.

Over time, constant responsiveness begins feeling normal.

People become accustomed to checking emails repeatedly, remaining mentally available after working hours, thinking about unfinished tasks late into the evening, and carrying low levels of stress throughout the day without fully recognizing how deeply it affects them.

This is one reason modern stress can feel difficult to identify clearly.

Many people are still functioning. But functioning is not the same as being internally balanced.

One of the clearest signs of chronic stress is the inability to fully relax even during moments of rest. You may sit down quietly, yet the mind continues thinking about what still needs attention. A conversation from earlier in the day replays repeatedly. Future responsibilities begin creating tension before they even arrive. The nervous system remains partially activated, preparing for problems that may not even exist in the present moment.

Over time, this continuous internal pressure begins affecting attention, emotional regulation, patience, sleep quality, energy levels, and overall mental clarity.

Small problems feel heavier. Emotional reactions become faster. Rest becomes less restorative. Even minor interruptions can begin creating disproportionate frustration or mental fatigue.

And because this condition develops gradually, many people stop questioning it altogether.

Stress becomes normalized. But the body and mind continue carrying the cost.

This is important to understand because modern stress is often less visible than traditional forms of pressure. It is not always dramatic or obvious. Sometimes it appears as constant mental occupation, emotional exhaustion, inability to disconnect, or the feeling that the mind is never fully at rest.

The system remains active even when the environment appears calm.

Awareness begins by recognizing this clearly.

Not every form of exhaustion comes from physical effort. Sometimes the deepest fatigue comes from remaining psychologically activated for too long without enough stillness, recovery, or emotional space to reset internally.

And when stress quietly becomes your normal state, balance slowly begins disappearing without you even noticing it happening.

Key Insights

- Cortisol helps the body respond to pressure, uncertainty, and stress.
- Modern life often keeps the nervous system continuously activated.
- Functioning normally does not always mean being mentally balanced.
- Chronic stress often appears as ongoing mental tension and inability to fully relax.
- Awareness begins by recognizing how long the mind has been carrying pressure without recovery.

SECTION 2: BURNOUT, MENTAL FATIGUE AND EMOTIONAL EXHAUSTION

Burnout rarely happens all at once.

For most people, it develops slowly through repeated periods of pressure, overstimulation, emotional strain, and insufficient recovery. At first, the signs are subtle. Energy feels slightly lower. Patience becomes shorter. Focus weakens more easily. Rest no longer feels fully restorative.

Over time, the mind begins carrying fatigue continuously.

One of the most difficult parts of burnout is that many people continue functioning while experiencing it. Work still gets completed. Responsibilities are still managed. Conversations continue normally. From the outside, life may appear stable and productive.

But internally, something begins changing.

Tasks that once felt manageable start feeling mentally heavier. Small interruptions create disproportionate frustration. Motivation becomes inconsistent. Emotional energy decreases. Even simple decisions can begin feeling exhausting after long periods of continuous mental pressure.

Many people respond to this state by pushing harder.

They try to become more productive, more disciplined, more efficient, or more available. But when the nervous system is already overloaded, increasing pressure often deepens exhaustion instead of resolving it.

This is why burnout is not simply about working too much.

It is often about remaining psychologically activated for too long without enough recovery, emotional space, or mental stillness.

Modern environments quietly intensify this condition. Constant accessibility, endless communication, digital overstimulation, performance expectations, and the pressure to remain continuously responsive prevent many people from fully disconnecting mentally. Even outside work, the mind often continues carrying unfinished conversations, future concerns, pending responsibilities, or emotional tension from earlier in the day.

As a result, recovery becomes incomplete.

The body may pause physically, but the mind continues working internally.

This creates a form of fatigue that rest alone does not always solve. A person may sleep for hours yet still wake up mentally tired. Free time may exist, yet genuine recovery still feels absent because attention never fully slows down long enough to reset deeply.

Emotional exhaustion often follows the same pattern.

When the nervous system remains under pressure continuously, emotional resilience gradually weakens. Patience becomes thinner. Small stressors feel larger. Emotional reactions become quicker and more automatic. Some people become irritable and restless. Others become emotionally numb, disconnected, or mentally withdrawn.

In many professional environments, this condition has quietly become normalized.

People remain busy constantly, respond quickly, multitask continuously, and stay mentally engaged throughout the day without recognizing how deeply prolonged activation affects emotional health over time. Productivity may continue externally while internal balance slowly deteriorates underneath.

One of the clearest signs of burnout is losing the ability to feel fully present in your own life.

The mind becomes occupied almost constantly — thinking ahead, recovering from pressure, managing stimulation, or carrying emotional tension from one moment into the next. Even enjoyable experiences may feel mentally distant because part of the nervous system never fully settles.

This is important to recognize because burnout is not always dramatic.

Sometimes it appears quietly through emotional depletion, mental fog, loss of enthusiasm, reduced focus, persistent fatigue, or the feeling that your internal energy is slowly disappearing faster than it can recover.

And when this state continues long enough, many people begin believing exhaustion is simply who they are.

But exhaustion is not identity.

It is often a signal that the mind and body have been carrying more pressure than they were designed to sustain continuously.

Awareness begins by recognizing that clearly.

Not with guilt or self-criticism, but with honesty.

Because once you understand how chronic pressure, overstimulation, and insufficient recovery shape your internal state, you begin seeing burnout not as personal weakness, but as a condition that develops when balance disappears for too long.

Key Insights

- Burnout develops gradually through prolonged pressure and insufficient recovery.
- Mental fatigue often continues even when external productivity remains high.
- Emotional exhaustion weakens patience, focus, and emotional resilience over time.
- Constant responsiveness and overstimulation make genuine recovery more difficult.
- Awareness helps recognize burnout before exhaustion becomes normalized.

SECTION 3: WHEN STRESS BECOMES YOUR NORMAL STATE

One of the most dangerous aspects of chronic stress is that people gradually stop recognizing it.

What begins as temporary pressure slowly becomes familiar. Constant mental occupation starts feeling normal. Emotional tension becomes part of everyday functioning. The mind remains busy so consistently that moments of genuine calm begin feeling unusual instead of natural.

This shift happens slowly.

At first, stress still feels temporary. A difficult week passes. Work becomes demanding. Responsibilities increase. Sleep becomes lighter. Attention feels more scattered. But eventually, many people stop expecting recovery completely. They adapt to carrying pressure continuously and begin treating ongoing stress as a normal part of adult life.

Over time, the nervous system adjusts to this state of constant activation.

The mind becomes conditioned toward alertness, anticipation, responsiveness, and mental movement. Even when external pressure decreases briefly, internal tension often continues because the system has spent so long preparing for the next demand, interruption, or responsibility.

This is why many people struggle to fully relax even when they finally have time to rest.

Silence may feel uncomfortable. Slowing down may create restlessness. Moments without stimulation or activity can begin feeling strangely unfamiliar because the mind has adapted to constant engagement for so long.

In some cases, people even become emotionally attached to busyness itself.

Being busy creates a sense of movement, importance, productivity, or distraction from unresolved discomfort underneath. As a result, slowing down can sometimes bring hidden exhaustion, emotional tension, or mental fatigue into awareness more clearly — which is why many people unconsciously avoid stillness altogether.

This pattern appears frequently in modern professional life.

Many individuals move continuously from one responsibility to another without fully recovering between them. Emails are checked during breaks. Conversations continue mentally after meetings end. Notifications interrupt attention repeatedly throughout the day. Even outside working hours, the mind often remains partially connected to unfinished tasks, future concerns, or the pressure to remain available.

The system rarely feels completely off.

Over time, this affects more than energy levels alone.

Chronic activation can gradually influence mood, emotional regulation, focus, sleep quality, decision-making, patience, and the ability to experience presence fully. Small stressors begin feeling heavier because the nervous system is already overloaded beneath the surface.

One of the clearest signs that stress has become normalized is when exhaustion no longer feels unusual.

People begin saying things like:

- "I'm always tired."
- "My mind never stops."
- "I can't relax properly anymore."
- "This is just how life is now."

And after enough repetition, they start believing it.

But constant stress is not the natural baseline of a healthy system.

Human beings are designed to move between activation and recovery. Stress itself is not the problem. The problem begins when recovery becomes incomplete while activation continues repeatedly for long periods of time.

This is where awareness becomes essential.

You begin recognizing that many feelings you assumed were permanent parts of your personality may actually be the result of prolonged mental and emotional overload. Restlessness, irritability, emotional numbness, difficulty focusing, and constant fatigue are not always personal flaws. Often, they are signals from a system that has remained activated for too long without enough balance.

Awareness does not remove stress from life completely.

But it changes the way you relate to it.

Instead of accepting constant exhaustion as normal, you begin noticing how your environment, habits, emotional patterns, and internal responses continuously shape your mental state throughout the day.

And sometimes, recognizing that you have been carrying stress for far too long is the first step toward finally allowing recovery to begin.

Key Insights

- Chronic stress often becomes normalized gradually over time.
- The nervous system can become conditioned to constant alertness and mental activity.
- Many people struggle to relax because the mind has adapted to continuous engagement.
- Emotional exhaustion often hides beneath constant busyness and productivity.
- Awareness helps recognize when stress has quietly become your normal state.

CHAPTER 4

THE DOPAMINE–CORTISOL CYCLE

SECTION 1: HOW STRESS FUELS STIMULATION

Stress and stimulation are often discussed as separate experiences.

But in everyday life, they are deeply connected.

One of the most common ways people respond to stress is by unconsciously moving toward stimulation. When the mind feels overwhelmed, emotionally tense, mentally tired, uncertain, or uncomfortable, attention naturally begins searching for something that provides relief, distraction, escape, or temporary emotional release.

Sometimes the shift is obvious.

Other times, it happens so quickly that people barely notice it.

A difficult task creates resistance, and attention suddenly moves toward checking messages. Emotional discomfort appears, and the mind begins searching for entertainment, food, stimulation, productivity, or distraction. Stress increases internally, and attention automatically looks for something that feels easier, lighter, or temporarily rewarding.

This is where dopamine and cortisol begin interacting continuously.

Cortisol increases alertness and internal pressure during stress. Dopamine then pulls attention toward behaviors associated with relief, anticipation, stimulation, or emotional escape. For a short time, the behavior may reduce tension or create temporary comfort.

But the relief rarely lasts very long.

Once the stimulation fades, the original pressure often returns underneath, which creates the urge to seek relief again. Over time, this cycle can repeat so frequently that it begins operating almost automatically.

Many people experience this pattern every day without fully recognizing it.

You may feel mentally overwhelmed and immediately search for distraction. You may move between tasks repeatedly instead of staying with difficult work long enough to complete it deeply. You may feel emotionally exhausted yet continue consuming stimulation late into the night because slowing down fully begins to feel uncomfortable.

The behavior often appears irrational from the outside.

But psychologically, the system is trying to regulate discomfort the fastest way it knows how.

This is one reason modern stress rarely remains purely emotional. It quickly becomes behavioral. Stress changes attention. Attention changes behavior. Behavior temporarily changes emotional state. And those repeated emotional shifts slowly condition long-term patterns.

This cycle appears far beyond digital distraction alone.

Some people respond to stress through constant busyness. Others seek productivity, achievement, shopping, entertainment, emotional eating, binge watching, validation, or continuous work without rest. The external behavior changes, but the underlying movement often remains similar:

moving away from discomfort and toward temporary relief.

In many professional environments, this cycle becomes especially difficult to recognize because stress-driven stimulation often appears productive. Constant responsiveness, multitasking, repeated email checking, and continuous mental engagement may feel efficient temporarily while quietly increasing long-term cognitive fatigue underneath.

The mind stays active continuously, but rarely fully settled.

Over time, this repeated interaction between stress and stimulation begins weakening the ability to remain present with discomfort calmly. The nervous system becomes increasingly conditioned toward immediate relief instead of emotional regulation, patience, recovery, or sustained attention.

This is why awareness becomes so important.

The moment you begin recognizing how stress influences your impulses, attention, and behaviors, the cycle becomes easier to observe clearly. You start noticing when the mind is genuinely choosing something intentionally and when it is simply reacting automatically to internal discomfort.

That recognition creates space.

And within that space, behavior slowly becomes more conscious instead of purely reactive.

Key Insights

- Stress often pushes attention toward stimulation and temporary relief.
- Dopamine and cortisol frequently reinforce each other in everyday behavior.

- Many distracting or compulsive behaviors are attempts to regulate discomfort quickly.
- Stress-driven stimulation can appear productive while increasing long-term fatigue.
- Awareness helps reveal the connection between emotional pressure and automatic behavior.

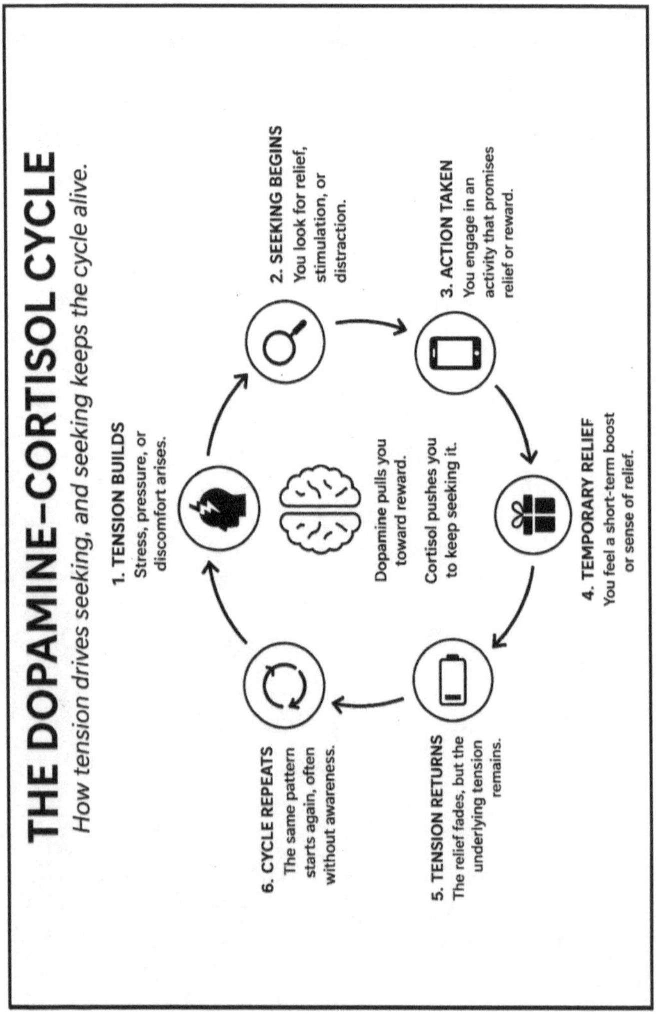
THE DOPAMINE–CORTISOL CYCLE
How tension drives seeking, and seeking keeps the cycle alive.
1. TENSION BUILDS
Stress, pressure, or discomfort arises.
2. SEEKING BEGINS
You look for relief, stimulation, or distraction.
3. ACTION TAKEN
You engage in an activity that promises relief or reward.
4. TEMPORARY RELIEF
You feel a short-term boost or sense of relief.
5. TENSION RETURNS
The relief fades, but the underlying tension remains.
6. CYCLE REPEATS
The same pattern starts again, often without awareness.
Dopamine pulls you toward reward.
Cortisol pushes you to keep seeking it.

SECTION 2: THE CYCLE IN EVERYDAY LIFE

The dopamine–cortisol cycle does not operate only during extreme situations.

It appears quietly throughout ordinary daily life.

Many people experience it repeatedly without fully noticing the pattern underneath their behavior. Stress, pressure, boredom, emotional discomfort, uncertainty, or mental fatigue create internal tension. Almost immediately, attention begins searching for relief through stimulation, distraction, movement, or emotional escape.

The reaction often feels automatic.

You sit down to complete an important task, but after a few minutes the mind begins searching for something easier or more stimulating. A notification suddenly feels difficult to ignore. Another tab gets opened. Messages are checked briefly. What started as a short distraction slowly turns into repeated interruptions that fragment attention for the rest of the day.

The original task remains unfinished.

And underneath the distraction, the pressure quietly continues.

This same pattern appears in many different forms.

Some people respond to stress through endless scrolling or entertainment. Others move toward excessive productivity, constant busyness, repeated email checking, emotional eating, online shopping, binge watching, or staying continuously occupied without allowing themselves genuine mental rest.

The external behavior changes.

But the internal movement often remains similar:

moving away from discomfort and toward temporary relief.

In professional environments, this cycle can become especially normalized. A difficult conversation creates emotional tension, so attention quickly shifts toward emails, meetings, notifications, or smaller tasks that feel easier to complete. Continuous activity creates the feeling of productivity while deeper mental fatigue quietly builds underneath.

Over time, many people stop noticing how reactive their attention has become.

The mind learns to escape discomfort quickly instead of remaining present with it long enough to process it calmly. Small moments of tension immediately trigger movement toward stimulation, distraction, or emotional relief. The nervous system begins expecting constant engagement whenever discomfort appears.

This affects more than focus alone.

Relationships become more distracted. Rest becomes less restorative. Conversations become shorter and more fragmented. Even enjoyable experiences may struggle to hold attention fully because the mind has become conditioned toward continuous movement and stimulation.

One of the clearest signs of this cycle is the inability to remain fully present during quiet moments.

Many people reach for stimulation automatically during waiting, boredom, loneliness, uncertainty, or emotional discomfort without consciously deciding to do so. The behavior feels natural because the cycle has been repeated so many times that it begins operating beneath awareness.

This is why the dopamine–cortisol cycle becomes so powerful.

Stress creates the desire for relief.

Relief is sought through stimulation. The stimulation temporarily changes emotional state.

But because the underlying pressure remains unresolved, the cycle eventually begins again.

And over time, repeated cycles slowly shape the way people think, feel, focus, rest, and experience everyday life itself.

Awareness begins when you start recognizing these moments clearly while they are happening.

Not afterward.

Not through guilt.

But in real time.

Because the moment you notice the mind automatically moving toward relief, distraction, or stimulation, you begin creating distance between the impulse and the reaction.

And that distance is where change slowly becomes possible.

Key Insights

- The dopamine–cortisol cycle appears repeatedly in everyday behavior.
- Many distractions are attempts to escape discomfort or mental tension temporarily.
- Stress-driven behaviors can appear productive while increasing internal fatigue.
- Repeated relief-seeking gradually conditions attention toward reactivity.

- Awareness begins by recognizing the cycle while it is happening in real time.

SECTION 3: BREAKING THE REWARD–STRESS PATTERN

Most people try to break unhealthy patterns by controlling behavior directly.

They force themselves to focus harder, remove distractions temporarily, create stricter routines, or depend on short bursts of motivation to stay disciplined. Sometimes these efforts help briefly. But when the deeper cycle underneath remains unchanged, the same behaviors often return again under stress, fatigue, boredom, or emotional pressure.

This is because the reward–stress cycle is not driven by behavior alone.

It is driven by conditioning.

Over time, the mind learns certain emotional patterns automatically. Stress creates discomfort. Discomfort creates the urge for relief. Relief is sought through stimulation, distraction, busyness, achievement, entertainment, or emotional escape. The temporary change in emotional state reinforces the pattern, making the same reaction more likely to repeat in the future.

The cycle becomes familiar.

And familiar patterns often feel natural even when they are unhealthy.

This is why breaking the cycle requires more than resisting urges repeatedly. Lasting change begins when you start recognizing the internal process happening before the behavior fully takes control.

Awareness creates that interruption.

You begin noticing the moment discomfort appears during focused work. You recognize when stress starts pulling attention toward distraction. You become aware of the emotional state underneath the craving instead of reacting automatically to the craving itself.

This changes something important.

For the first time, the mind begins observing the pattern instead of moving unconsciously inside it.

That observation creates space between impulse and reaction.

And within that space, different responses slowly become possible.

Instead of immediately escaping discomfort, you begin staying present with it slightly longer. Instead of reacting automatically to every urge for stimulation, you begin recognizing that not every impulse requires action. Instead of treating stress as something that must instantly disappear, you begin understanding how to experience discomfort without immediately moving toward relief.

This is not about becoming perfectly disciplined or eliminating stimulation completely.

It is about rebuilding intentional attention.

Small moments of awareness matter more than most people realize. Noticing the urge to check something without immediately acting on it. Remaining present with difficult work for a few extra minutes before seeking distraction. Allowing silence, boredom, or stillness to exist briefly without automatically filling the space.

These moments slowly retrain attention.

Over time, the nervous system becomes less dependent on constant stimulation for emotional regulation. Focus strengthens gradually. Emotional reactions slow down. Stillness becomes less uncomfortable. The mind begins recovering the ability to remain present without continuously searching for relief.

This process is not immediate.

Patterns built through years of repetition do not disappear overnight. Some days the cycle will still feel automatic. Stress will still create urges. Distraction will still appear tempting. But awareness changes the relationship with those impulses even before behavior changes fully.

And that shift matters deeply.

Because freedom does not begin when every craving disappears.

It begins when you are no longer completely controlled by every impulse that appears.

Breaking the reward–stress pattern is ultimately not about fighting yourself constantly.

It is about understanding yourself clearly enough to stop living entirely on automatic.

Key Insights

- Lasting change requires understanding the cycle beneath behavior.
- Awareness creates space between impulse and automatic reaction.
- Small moments of conscious attention gradually retrain the nervous system.
- Emotional discomfort does not always need immediate relief or distraction.
- Breaking the cycle begins by becoming less reactive to every impulse.

CHAPTER 5

FROM REACTIVITY TO AWARENESS

SECTION 1: THE AWARENESS GAP

Most people believe they are fully aware of their own behavior.

But much of everyday life is lived automatically.

Thoughts appear quickly. Reactions happen instantly. Attention shifts constantly. Habits repeat themselves so naturally that many behaviors begin operating beneath conscious awareness long before people fully notice what they are doing.

This is the awareness gap.

It is the space between what is happening internally and what you consciously recognize while it is happening.

The awareness gap explains why people often repeat behaviors they genuinely want to change. A person may promise themselves they will stay focused, avoid distractions, rest properly, or respond more calmly under stress. Yet moments later, attention drifts automatically toward old patterns again before conscious awareness fully catches up.

The reaction happens first.

Awareness arrives later.

This gap exists because the brain is designed to conserve energy through automatic behavior. Repeated thoughts, emotional reactions, habits, and coping patterns gradually become conditioned over time. The more often something is repeated, the less conscious attention the brain requires to continue doing it.

This is useful in many situations.

Without automatic behavior, even simple daily tasks would require exhausting amounts of mental effort. But the same system that creates efficiency can also reinforce unhealthy emotional and behavioral patterns when they remain unexamined for too long.

Over time, people stop noticing many of their automatic reactions completely.

Stress creates irritation before awareness notices tension building. Boredom triggers stimulation - seeking before the mind recognizes discomfort. Emotional pressure leads to distraction, avoidance, or overconsumption before conscious thought fully understands what is happening internally.

This is why so many behaviors feel difficult to control through willpower alone.

You cannot consciously interrupt a pattern that you do not notice while it is happening.

The awareness gap becomes especially powerful in modern environments because attention is constantly pulled outward. Notifications, responsibilities, stimulation, information, and continuous engagement leave very little space for people to observe their own internal state clearly. Many individuals spend entire days reacting without pausing long enough to notice what their mind and body are actually experiencing underneath the activity.

As a result, automatic living slowly becomes normalized.

People continue functioning, working, responding, consuming, and staying busy while losing deeper awareness of:

- their emotional state,
- mental fatigue,
- internal tension,
- behavioral patterns,
- and the unconscious impulses driving many of their decisions.

One of the clearest signs of the awareness gap is the feeling of suddenly "waking up" inside a behavior after it has already been happening for some time.

You realize you have been scrolling without intention.

You notice your mind replaying stress repeatedly.

You become aware that you reacted emotionally before fully understanding why.

You recognize exhaustion only after the body has already been under pressure for too long.

In these moments, awareness briefly returns.

And that moment matters more than most people realize.

Because awareness is not about becoming perfectly controlled.

It is about becoming conscious enough to see what was previously operating automatically.

The moment a pattern becomes visible, your relationship with it begins changing. The behavior may still appear. The impulses may still exist. But awareness creates distance between you and the automatic reaction itself.

That distance is where intentional change begins.

Not through force.

Not through self-criticism.

But through seeing clearly.

Because once you begin recognizing your internal patterns in real time, you stop living completely on autopilot.

And that is where deeper transformation quietly starts.

Key Insights

- Many behaviors operate automatically beneath conscious awareness.
- The awareness gap is the space between reaction and conscious recognition.
- Repeated patterns become difficult to change when they remain unconscious.
- Modern life keeps attention externally occupied, reducing self-observation.
- Awareness begins when you notice patterns while they are happening.

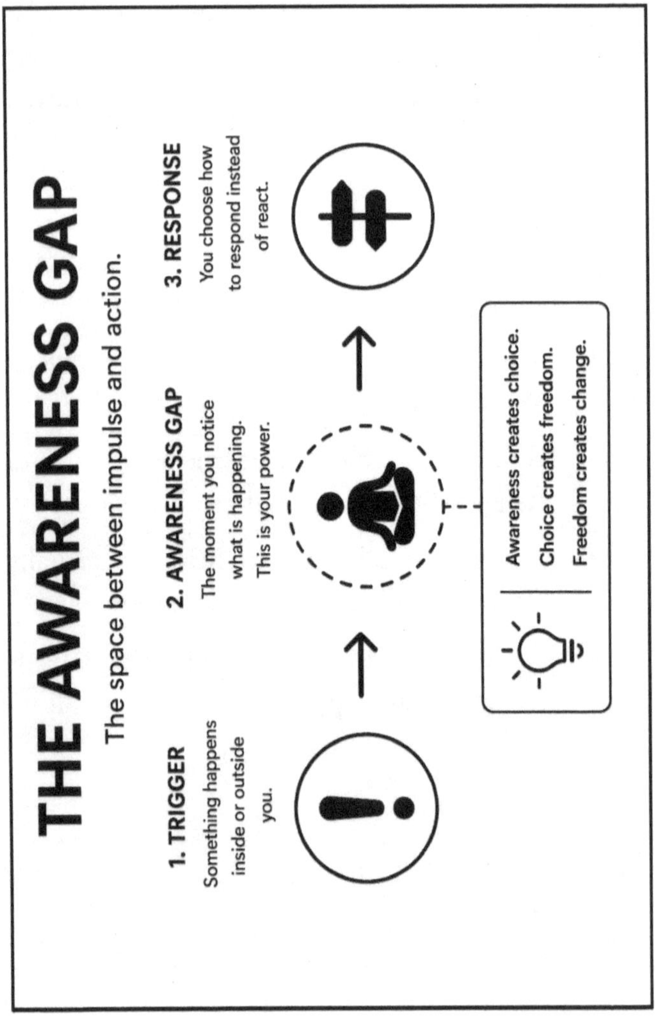
THE AWARENESS GAP
The space between impulse and action.
1. TRIGGER
Something happens inside or outside you.
2. AWARENESS GAP
The moment you notice what is happening. This is your power.
3. RESPONSE
You choose how to respond instead of react.
Awareness creates choice.
Choice creates freedom.
Freedom creates change.

SECTION 2: RECOGNIZING YOUR INTERNAL PATTERNS

Most people spend far more time reacting to their thoughts, emotions, and impulses than observing them.

Reactions happen quickly. Stress creates tension. Discomfort creates avoidance. Emotional pressure changes behavior. Attention moves automatically toward stimulation, distraction, or relief before the deeper pattern underneath is fully recognized.

Over time, these reactions begin feeling natural simply because they happen so often.

But awareness grows through observation.

The moment you begin paying attention to your internal patterns consistently, certain behaviors that once felt random begin revealing clear emotional and psychological connections underneath them.

You start noticing what triggers distraction.

You recognize which situations increase emotional tension.

You observe how stress changes your attention.

You begin seeing how certain emotions repeatedly influence specific behaviors.

What once felt automatic starts becoming visible.

This process is important because many people attempt to change behavior without first understanding the emotional patterns driving it. They focus only on controlling actions externally while remaining disconnected from the internal states that repeatedly produce those actions in the first place.

But behavior is often a response to something deeper.

A person may seek stimulation because they feel emotionally overwhelmed.

They may overwork because stillness feels uncomfortable.

They may avoid difficult tasks because stress triggers mental resistance.

They may stay constantly busy because slowing down brings unresolved exhaustion into awareness.

Without recognizing the pattern underneath, the behavior itself continues repeating automatically.

This is why self-observation matters more deeply than many people realize.

Awareness is not simply noticing external habits.

It is learning to observe:

- emotional reactions,
- mental tension,
- attention shifts,
- internal discomfort,
- stress responses,
- and repeated psychological movements beneath behavior itself.

One of the most powerful changes begins when you stop immediately identifying with every thought, emotion, or impulse that appears.

Instead of: "I need to escape this feeling."

You begin noticing: "My mind is searching for relief right now."

That small shift changes your relationship with yourself.

You begin observing your internal state instead of becoming completely absorbed inside it.

This does not mean emotions disappear immediately.

Stress may still appear.

Discomfort may still arise.

Old impulses may still feel strong.

But awareness creates a pause between the feeling and the automatic reaction. And within that pause, patterns that once controlled behavior unconsciously begin losing some of their power.

Many people never develop this kind of self-observation because modern life leaves very little space for internal awareness. Attention remains focused outward almost constantly — toward responsibilities, stimulation, information, deadlines, conversations, entertainment, and external demands.

As a result, people often understand the external world better than they understand themselves.

Recognizing your internal patterns changes that.

You begin seeing how your nervous system responds to stress.

You notice what drains your attention.

You recognize the emotional states driving many of your habits.

And slowly, your reactions become easier to understand with greater clarity and less self-judgment.

This is where awareness becomes transformative.

Not because it creates instant perfection, but because it helps you stop living completely unconsciously inside patterns you never fully noticed before.

The more clearly you observe yourself, the more intentionally you begin responding to life instead of reacting automatically to it.

Key Insights

- Awareness grows through observing internal patterns consistently.
- Many behaviors are emotional responses operating beneath conscious thought.
- Self-observation creates distance between emotions and automatic reactions.
- Understanding internal patterns reduces unconscious living and self-judgment.
- The more clearly you observe yourself, the more intentionally you can respond.

SECTION 3: THE POWER OF CONSCIOUS ATTENTION

Attention is one of the most powerful forces shaping human experience.

Whatever repeatedly captures your attention gradually influences your thoughts, emotions, habits, relationships, energy, and overall mental state. Over time, attention does not simply determine what you focus on temporarily. It shapes how you experience life itself.

Most people rarely notice where their attention is being directed throughout the day.

The mind moves automatically from one thought to another, one responsibility to another, one source of stimulation to another without much conscious awareness guiding the process. External demands, emotional reactions, stress, habits, and digital environments continuously compete for attention, often pulling it in multiple directions at the same time.

As a result, many people live with fragmented awareness.

Part of the mind remains attached to unfinished work.

Another part replays past conversations.

Another anticipates future problems.

Another searches for stimulation or relief.

Attention becomes divided so frequently that sustained presence begins feeling increasingly rare.

This is why conscious attention matters so deeply.

Conscious attention is the ability to intentionally notice where your awareness is moving instead of allowing every impulse, distraction, emotion, or external demand to control it automatically. It is not about forcing perfect concentration at all times. It is about becoming more aware of what repeatedly receives your mental energy throughout daily life.

This changes something important internally.

The moment attention becomes more conscious, automatic patterns begin losing some of their control. You start noticing when stress is pulling you toward distraction. You recognize when emotional discomfort is influencing your decisions. You become aware of how certain environments, conversations, habits, or thought patterns affect your mental state throughout the day.

Attention slowly becomes intentional instead of purely reactive.

This shift often begins through very small moments.

Remaining fully present during a conversation instead of mentally multitasking.

Noticing the urge to check something without immediately acting on it.

Completing one task before moving automatically toward another.

Allowing moments of silence without rushing to fill them with stimulation.

These moments may appear insignificant.

But repeated conscious attention gradually retrains the nervous system.

Over time, the mind becomes less dependent on constant stimulation and more capable of sustained focus, emotional regulation, and internal stability. Stillness begins feeling less uncomfortable. Thoughts slow down slightly. Reactions become less immediate. The mind starts recovering the ability to remain present instead of constantly pulled outward.

This does not mean life becomes stress-free or perfectly controlled.

Distractions will still exist.

Pressure will still appear.

Difficult emotions will still arise.

But conscious attention changes your relationship with those experiences.

Instead of being pulled automatically in every direction, you begin developing the ability to observe, choose, and respond more intentionally. Attention becomes something you guide more consciously instead of something the environment continuously controls for you.

In many ways, this is where awareness becomes practical.

Not as an abstract idea, but as a daily way of living with greater clarity, presence, and internal balance.

Because wherever your attention repeatedly goes, your life slowly follows.

And when attention becomes more conscious, life itself begins feeling more intentional.

Key Insights

- Attention gradually shapes thoughts, emotions, habits, and daily experience.
- Modern life continuously fragments awareness and pulls attention outward.

- Conscious attention helps reduce automatic and reactive behavior.
- Small moments of presence gradually retrain the nervous system.
- Where attention repeatedly goes, your mental and emotional life slowly follows.

CHAPTER 6

MASTERING YOUR INTERNAL SYSTEMS

SECTION 1: REGULATING DOPAMINE - REBALANCING THE PULL

Dopamine itself is not the problem.

Human beings need dopamine to feel motivated, engaged, curious, creative, and emotionally connected to life. Without it, pursuing goals, learning new skills, building relationships, or finding meaning in everyday experiences would become extremely difficult.

The issue begins when the mind becomes overstimulated continuously.

Modern environments expose people to an endless stream of novelty, anticipation, entertainment, information, and emotional stimulation. Over time, the nervous system gradually adapts to high levels of engagement and begins expecting frequent reward, movement, and stimulation throughout the day.

As this pattern strengthens, quieter experiences often begin feeling less satisfying by comparison.

Simple activities that once felt calming or meaningful may start feeling "too slow." Sustained focus becomes harder. Patience weakens more quickly. The mind increasingly searches for stronger stimulation, faster engagement, or more immediate emotional reward.

This is how imbalance develops gradually.

The nervous system becomes conditioned toward constant seeking.

Many people notice this pattern without fully understanding it. They struggle to remain present with one task for long periods. Silence feels uncomfortable. Rest quickly turns into stimulation. Moments of boredom immediately trigger the urge to check, consume, switch, scroll, or engage with something else.

The mind keeps searching because it has adapted to continuous input.

Regulating dopamine does not mean removing pleasure from life or avoiding all stimulation completely. The goal is not restriction for its own sake. The goal is restoring balance between stimulation and recovery so the nervous system no longer depends on constant engagement to feel emotionally regulated.

This begins by becoming more intentional about what repeatedly captures your attention.

Not every impulse needs immediate response.

Not every moment of boredom needs stimulation.

Not every emotional discomfort needs instant escape.

Small moments of pause begin retraining attention gradually.

You start spending slightly longer with difficult work before seeking distraction. You allow moments of stillness without automatically filling them. You become more aware of how certain environments, habits, and behaviors affect your mental clarity and emotional state afterward.

Over time, something important begins changing internally.

The mind becomes less reactive to every urge for stimulation. Focus strengthens gradually. Slower experiences become easier to tolerate again. Attention feels less scattered because the nervous system is no longer being pushed toward constant novelty at the same intensity.

This process also changes motivation.

When dopamine becomes more balanced, motivation starts feeling less dependent on emotional highs, instant rewards, or constant excitement. The mind becomes more capable of engaging with meaningful activities even when they are slower, quieter, or mentally demanding.

This is important because many of the most valuable parts of life develop slowly:

- deep relationships
- meaningful work
- emotional stability
- creativity
- reflection
- learning
- and inner clarity

These experiences rarely compete with the speed and intensity of modern stimulation.

They require attention that is calm enough to stay present.

Regulating dopamine is ultimately about rebuilding that ability.

Not through force or extreme discipline, but through gradually reducing automatic dependence on constant stimulation and becoming more intentional about how attention is used every day.

Because when the nervous system no longer feels pulled continuously in every direction, the mind slowly begins recovering something modern life often takes away quietly.

Key Insights

- Dopamine imbalance develops through continuous overstimulation and constant novelty.
- The nervous system gradually becomes conditioned toward frequent reward and stimulation.
- Regulating dopamine is about restoring balance, not eliminating pleasure.
- Small moments of pause and intentional attention slowly retrain the mind.
- Lasting focus and emotional clarity grow when attention becomes less reactive.

SECTION 2: CALMING CORTISOL — RESTORING STABILITY

Stress cannot be removed completely from life.

Challenges, uncertainty, responsibilities, pressure, and emotional difficulty are natural parts of being human. The goal is not to eliminate stress entirely, but to prevent the nervous system from remaining trapped in continuous activation without enough recovery.

This is where calming cortisol becomes important.

Many people now live in a state where the mind rarely feels fully settled. Even during rest, part of the nervous system often remains alert — thinking ahead, anticipating problems, replaying conversations, managing unfinished responsibilities, or searching for stimulation to avoid emotional discomfort.

Over time, constant activation begins feeling normal.

But the body continues carrying the effects internally.

Calming cortisol is not simply about relaxation techniques or temporary stress reduction. It is about helping the nervous system experience safety, stillness, recovery, and emotional regulation more consistently throughout daily life.

This process begins with recognizing how much unnecessary activation modern environments create.

- Constant responsiveness.
- Continuous multitasking.
- Information overload.
- Emotional overstimulation.
- Pressure to remain available.
- Lack of mental recovery.
- Insufficient sleep.
- Endless engagement without stillness.

The nervous system absorbs all of it.

And when activation continues for too long without enough balance, emotional resilience gradually weakens. Small problems begin feeling heavier. Patience decreases more quickly. Rest becomes less restorative. The mind starts reacting to life from exhaustion instead of stability.

This is why recovery must become intentional.

Many people assume recovery simply means stopping work temporarily. But genuine recovery requires more than physical rest alone. The nervous system also needs moments where attention slows down, emotional pressure decreases, and the mind no longer feels constantly pulled toward stimulation, urgency, or anticipation.

Sometimes recovery looks very simple.

- Quiet moments without digital engagement.
- Walking without constant mental occupation.
- Completing one task slowly without multitasking.
- Sitting with your thoughts without immediately escaping into stimulation.

Allowing the body and mind to experience stillness without filling every empty space.

These moments may appear small externally.

But internally, they teach the nervous system that constant activation is not necessary for survival.

Over time, this changes emotional regulation significantly.

- The mind becomes less reactive.
- Stress responses slow down slightly.
- Attention feels more stable.
- Emotional overwhelm decreases more easily.

The body begins recovering its ability to move between activation and calmness more naturally.

This process also changes the relationship people have with productivity.

Many individuals unconsciously associate constant busyness with value, progress, or control. Slowing down can initially feel uncomfortable because stillness allows hidden exhaustion and emotional tension to become more visible.

But avoiding stillness does not remove exhaustion. It only delays awareness of it.

Calming cortisol often requires relearning something modern life continuously interrupts: the ability to feel safe without constant mental activity. This does not happen instantly.

The nervous system adapts gradually through repeated experiences of recovery, balance, emotional regulation, and conscious attention. Small changes repeated consistently often influence long-term stability more deeply than extreme short-term efforts.

This is why awareness remains central throughout the process.

The more clearly you recognize what continuously activates your nervous system, the more intentionally you can begin creating environments, habits, and behaviors that support emotional balance instead of constant internal pressure. Because a calm mind is not created through force.

It develops when the nervous system finally experiences enough space to stop fighting for relief constantly.

Key Insights

- Chronic stress develops when activation continues without enough recovery.
- Genuine recovery requires mental and emotional stillness, not only physical rest.
- Constant busyness often hides deeper exhaustion and emotional tension.
- Small moments of calm and intentional slowing down retrain the nervous system gradually.
- Emotional stability grows when the mind no longer lives in continuous activation.

SECTION 3: REBUILDING ATTENTION AND MENTAL CLARITY

One of the most noticeable effects of prolonged overstimulation and chronic stress is the gradual weakening of attention.

Many people now live with minds that feel constantly occupied. Thoughts move quickly. Focus shifts repeatedly. Mental energy becomes scattered across responsibilities, stimulation, worries, notifications, unfinished tasks, and emotional pressure throughout the day.

As a result, clarity begins fading slowly.

This does not always appear dramatically at first. Sometimes it shows up as difficulty concentrating deeply for long periods. Sometimes it feels like mental fog, emotional overload, forgetfulness, restlessness, or the inability to remain fully present with one thing without the urge to shift attention elsewhere.

Over time, the mind becomes accustomed to fragmentation.

Attention starts reacting automatically to whatever feels most urgent, stimulating, emotionally charged, or immediately rewarding. Deep focus becomes harder not because the brain has lost its ability to concentrate, but because the nervous system has spent too long adapting to interruption, speed, and continuous mental movement.

This is why rebuilding attention requires more than productivity techniques alone.

It requires creating conditions where the mind can gradually recover its ability to slow down, settle, and engage more intentionally again.

The process begins by reducing unnecessary fragmentation.

Many people attempt to focus while continuously dividing attention between multiple tasks, conversations, devices, thoughts, and emotional pressures at the same time. The mind remains partially attached to several things simultaneously, which quietly drains cognitive energy throughout the day.

Attention weakens when it is repeatedly scattered.

Clarity strengthens when attention becomes more deliberate.

This is why small shifts matter.

- Completing one task fully before switching to another.
- Allowing periods without constant stimulation.
- Creating moments where attention is not continuously interrupted.
- Spending time in environments that feel mentally calmer instead of emotionally overloaded.

These actions may appear simple externally.

But internally, they begin retraining the nervous system toward steadiness instead of constant reactivity.

One of the most important parts of rebuilding mental clarity is relearning how to stay present with slower experiences again.

- Reading carefully.
- Thinking deeply.
- Listening fully during conversations.
- Working without immediately escaping discomfort.

- Allowing quiet moments without filling every space with stimulation.

At first, these experiences may feel uncomfortable because the mind has adapted to speed and continuous engagement for so long. Restlessness may appear quickly. Attention may keep searching for novelty. The urge to switch focus may feel strong.

This is normal.

The nervous system is adjusting.

Over time, consistent periods of intentional attention gradually strengthen mental stability again. Thoughts become less scattered. Emotional overwhelm decreases more easily. Focus lasts longer. The mind begins recovering its ability to remain engaged without needing constant stimulation to stay active.

This also changes emotional experience.

When attention becomes calmer, people often feel more emotionally grounded, less reactive, and more connected to their surroundings. Conversations feel more meaningful. Rest becomes more restorative. Daily life begins feeling less rushed internally even when responsibilities still exist externally.

Mental clarity is not created through forcing the mind aggressively.

It develops when attention is no longer being continuously pulled in every direction at once.

This is why rebuilding attention is ultimately not just about productivity.

It is about restoring the ability to experience life with greater presence, steadiness, and intentional awareness.

Because when attention becomes clearer, the mind slowly begins feeling like a place you can rest inside again instead of constantly trying to escape from.

Key Insights

- Chronic stress and overstimulation gradually weaken sustained attention.
- Mental clarity improves when attention becomes less fragmented and reactive.
- Small moments of intentional focus slowly retrain the nervous system.
- Slower experiences help rebuild steadiness, presence, and cognitive balance.
- Rebuilding attention is not only about productivity, but about restoring internal stability.

SECTION 4: CREATING INTERNAL BALANCE THROUGH AWARENESS

Many people spend years trying to control their external life while remaining disconnected from their internal state.

They organize schedules, improve productivity, manage responsibilities, and chase goals continuously, yet still feel mentally restless, emotionally exhausted, or internally overwhelmed underneath. The external structure may improve, but the nervous system often continues carrying stress, overstimulation, and unconscious reactivity beneath the surface.

This is why balance cannot be created only externally.

Real balance begins internally.

Internal balance is not the absence of stress, difficulty, emotion, or challenge. It is the ability to remain more aware, stable, and intentional while moving through those experiences instead of becoming completely controlled by them automatically.

Awareness is what makes that possible.

Without awareness, most reactions happen unconsciously. Stress changes behavior before it is recognized. Emotional discomfort creates impulsive responses. Attention gets pulled toward distraction, stimulation, urgency, or relief automatically. People continue reacting to internal pressure without fully understanding what is shaping their behavior underneath.

Awareness changes the relationship with those patterns.

The moment you begin observing your internal state more clearly, you start noticing:

- what activates your nervous system,
- what drains your attention,
- what repeatedly creates emotional tension,
- and what genuinely restores mental clarity and stability.

This understanding becomes deeply important because many people attempt to build balanced lives while continuing habits that quietly keep the nervous system overstimulated and emotionally overloaded every day.

Awareness helps reveal those contradictions.

- You begin recognizing when busyness is becoming emotional escape.
- When stimulation is replacing recovery.
- When productivity is turning into avoidance.
- When exhaustion is being normalized instead of acknowledged honestly.

These realizations are not always comfortable. But they are necessary.

Because lasting balance cannot develop through unconscious living.

It grows through consistent self-observation and intentional adjustment over time.

This process is rarely dramatic.

Internal balance is often rebuilt through small repeated shifts:

- creating more space for recovery,
- reducing unnecessary stimulation,
- slowing reactive behavior,
- becoming more present during daily experiences,
- and learning to respond consciously instead of automatically.

At first, these changes may feel subtle.

But over time, the nervous system begins responding differently.

- Stress no longer controls attention as easily.
- Discomfort becomes more tolerable without immediate escape.
- The mind feels less scattered.
- Emotional reactions slow down slightly.
- Stillness becomes less uncomfortable.
- Presence becomes easier to access.

This is where awareness moves beyond theory and becomes a lived experience.

You stop trying to force yourself into constant control and begin understanding how to work with your nervous system more intelligently and compassionately instead of against it.

That shift changes more than habits alone.

It changes the way you experience everyday life.

Balance stops feeling like something distant that only exists after everything becomes perfect externally. Instead, it becomes something built gradually through awareness, intentional attention, emotional honesty, and the ability to recognize when your internal state is moving too far away from stability.

This does not create a perfect life.

But it creates a more conscious one.

And over time, that awareness becomes one of the most powerful forms of stability a person can develop in a distracted and overstimulated world.

Key Insights

- Real balance begins through awareness of internal patterns and reactions.
- Many people manage external responsibilities while remaining internally overloaded.
- Awareness helps reveal behaviors that quietly increase overstimulation and exhaustion.
- Small intentional shifts gradually rebuild emotional and mental stability.
- Internal balance develops through conscious living, not constant control.

CHAPTER 7

THE MODERN ENVIRONMENT: DESIGNED TO CAPTURE YOU

SECTION 1: THE ATTENTION ECONOMY

Human attention has become one of the most valuable resources in the modern world.

Entire industries now compete continuously for it.

Technology platforms, media systems, advertising networks, entertainment companies, and digital environments are all designed around one central objective: keeping people engaged for as long as possible.

This is the foundation of the attention economy.

The longer attention stays captured, the more valuable it becomes commercially. As a result, modern environments are carefully engineered to encourage repeated engagement, emotional reaction, anticipation, stimulation, and continuous interaction throughout the day.

Most people do not fully recognize how deeply this shapes everyday experience.

Attention is constantly being pulled toward notifications, headlines, recommendations, trending content, updates, advertisements, messages, alerts, and endless streams of information competing simultaneously for mental space. The mind rarely gets an opportunity to settle before another stimulus appears demanding attention again.

Over time, this repeated interruption changes behavior.

The nervous system gradually adapts to speed, novelty, emotional stimulation, and constant movement. Quiet moments become shorter. Patience weakens more easily. Deep focus becomes more difficult to maintain because attention is repeatedly trained toward interruption and rapid shifting.

The environment itself begins shaping the way the mind functions.

This influence extends far beyond social media alone.

Modern life continuously encourages responsiveness:

- answer quickly,
- react immediately,
- stay updated,
- remain available,

- keep consuming,
- keep engaging,
- keep moving.

In many professional environments, this pressure becomes even stronger. Responsiveness is often rewarded more visibly than deep focus. People feel expected to remain reachable, informed, productive, and mentally available almost constantly. As a result, many individuals spend entire days reacting to incoming demands without enough uninterrupted space for deeper thinking, emotional recovery, or mental stillness.

The nervous system rarely experiences true disengagement.

One of the most important things to understand about the attention economy is that it does not only compete for time.

It competes for emotional energy.

Content that creates stronger emotional reactions often captures attention more effectively. Fear, outrage, comparison, urgency, novelty, validation, and stimulation keep people engaged longer because emotionally activated minds are easier to hold inside continuous cycles of interaction.

Over time, this affects more than productivity or focus alone.

It influences mood, emotional regulation, patience, relationships, self-perception, and even the ability to remain present during ordinary life experiences. Attention becomes externally directed so consistently that many people gradually lose connection with their own internal state underneath the constant engagement.

This is why awareness becomes essential in modern environments.

Without awareness, people often assume their mental exhaustion, restlessness, distraction, or emotional overstimulation are simply personal weaknesses. But many of these experiences are strongly influenced by environments intentionally designed to capture and hold attention continuously.

Recognizing this changes perspective.

You begin understanding that protecting attention is no longer only about discipline.

It is about creating conscious boundaries inside systems specifically designed to weaken them.

This does not mean rejecting technology or modern life completely.

It means learning to engage with the environment more intentionally instead of allowing every external demand to shape your attention automatically.

Because whatever repeatedly captures your attention gradually shapes your mental and emotional life over time.

And in a world constantly competing for attention, conscious awareness becomes a form of protection.

Key Insights

- Modern environments are designed to continuously capture and hold attention.
- The attention economy profits from repeated engagement and emotional stimulation.
- Constant responsiveness weakens deep focus, recovery, and mental stillness over time.
- Attention is influenced not only by technology, but by broader cultural and workplace expectations.
- Awareness helps create intentional boundaries within overstimulating environments.

SECTION 2: HOW DIGITAL ENVIRONMENTS SHAPE BEHAVIOR

Human behavior is shaped not only by personal choices, but also by the environments people spend time inside every day.

Over time, environments quietly influence attention, habits, emotional responses, decision-making, and even the way people think about themselves without those changes always being consciously recognized.

Digital environments are especially powerful in this regard because they interact with the brain continuously.

Unlike older forms of media that demanded attention only occasionally, modern digital systems remain active throughout the day. Phones stay nearby constantly. Notifications interrupt attention repeatedly. Algorithms continuously learn preferences, emotional reactions, and behavioral patterns in order to keep engagement active for longer periods of time.

As a result, many people are no longer simply using digital environments.

They are living inside them psychologically.

This changes behavior gradually.

- Attention becomes more reactive.
- Patience weakens more quickly.
- Silence feels uncomfortable.

The urge to check, refresh, switch, respond, or consume begins appearing automatically throughout the day.

Most people do not consciously decide to behave this way repeatedly.

The environment conditions the behavior through constant exposure.

One of the most powerful aspects of digital environments is their ability to shape emotional states quickly. A single notification can change attention instantly. Comparison-driven content can influence mood within seconds. News cycles can create continuous emotional activation. Validation through likes, messages, or responses can temporarily influence self-worth and emotional regulation without people fully noticing the effect internally.

Over time, the nervous system adapts to this constant emotional movement.

The mind begins expecting:

- stimulation,
- updates,
- interaction,
- novelty,
- and responsiveness continuously.

This makes slower experiences increasingly difficult to tolerate. Deep reading, focused work, quiet reflection, and uninterrupted presence may begin feeling mentally uncomfortable not because they lack value, but because the nervous system has adapted to faster emotional and cognitive rhythms.

This conditioning also influences relationships and communication.

Many conversations now compete with devices, notifications, and divided attention. People may physically spend time together while mentally remaining connected to multiple external streams of stimulation simultaneously. Presence becomes fragmented because attention rarely settles fully in one place for long.

In professional life, digital environments often intensify pressure further.

Constant communication systems create the expectation of ongoing responsiveness. Many individuals feel mentally connected to work long after working hours end because messages, updates, and notifications continue entering attention repeatedly throughout the day and night. Recovery becomes more difficult when the nervous system never fully disconnects from engagement.

One of the most important realities to understand is that digital environments are not neutral.

They are intentionally designed to shape behavior.

Every alert, recommendation, autoplay feature, endless feed, and engagement mechanism is built to increase interaction and maintain attention for longer periods. The system works most effectively when behavior becomes automatic enough that people stop consciously questioning how much attention they are giving away.

This is why awareness matters so deeply.

The more clearly you observe how environments influence your attention, emotions, habits, and mental state, the more intentionally you can begin choosing how you engage with them instead of reacting automatically to every stimulus presented to you.

Because environments shape behavior quietly.

And when awareness is absent, people often mistake conditioned behavior for personal choice.

Key Insights

- Digital environments continuously shape attention, habits, emotions, and behavior.
- Constant exposure to stimulation gradually conditions the nervous system toward reactivity.
- Modern digital systems influence emotional states through validation, novelty, urgency, and comparison.
- Continuous connectivity makes deep focus, recovery, and presence more difficult.
- Awareness helps people engage with digital environments more intentionally instead of automatically.

SECTION 3: CREATING SPACE WITHIN A DISTRACTED WORLD

Modern life rarely leaves empty space.

Attention is constantly occupied by information, responsibilities, stimulation, communication, entertainment, and emotional input flowing continuously throughout the day. Even moments that once allowed mental recovery — waiting quietly, walking alone, sitting without activity, or resting without interruption — are now often filled immediately with screens, updates, content, or mental engagement.

As a result, many people no longer experience true psychological space.

The mind remains active almost constantly.

This continuous engagement creates an important problem: when attention never slows down, awareness becomes weaker.

People lose the ability to notice what they are feeling internally because the nervous system remains focused outward continuously. Stress gets buried beneath activity. Emotional exhaustion hides beneath busyness. Mental fatigue becomes difficult to recognize because stimulation keeps temporarily masking it.

The environment stays loud enough that deeper internal signals are rarely heard clearly.

This is why creating intentional space becomes so important.

Not because silence itself solves every problem, but because awareness becomes much harder when the mind is continuously overwhelmed by stimulation, urgency, and distraction.

Creating space means allowing attention to breathe again.

It means reducing unnecessary mental noise long enough to reconnect with:

- your thoughts,
- emotional state,
- nervous system,
- attention patterns,
- and internal experience more clearly.

For many people, this initially feels uncomfortable.

The moment external stimulation decreases, hidden restlessness often becomes more noticeable. Thoughts feel louder. Emotional tension surfaces more clearly. The urge to reach for distraction appears quickly because the nervous system has become accustomed to constant engagement for so long.

This reaction is normal.

The mind has adapted to stimulation as a way of avoiding stillness, discomfort, uncertainty, or emotional fatigue. When space finally appears, the nervous system temporarily struggles to settle because it is no longer being continuously occupied.

But this is also where recovery begins.

Small moments of intentional space slowly retrain attention.

Walking without constant input.

Sitting quietly for a few minutes.

Working without switching tasks repeatedly.

Allowing conversations without divided attention.

Reducing unnecessary stimulation before sleep.

Spending time without constantly consuming information.

These moments may appear insignificant externally.

But internally, they help the nervous system recover its ability to slow down, regulate emotion, and remain present without needing continuous stimulation to feel stable.

Creating space also changes the relationship people have with themselves.

When the environment becomes quieter, patterns that were previously hidden often become easier to recognize. You begin noticing what genuinely drains your energy. You see how certain habits affect your emotional state. You recognize when busyness becomes avoidance and when stimulation is replacing real recovery.

Awareness becomes clearer because the mind finally has enough space to observe itself again.

This does not require abandoning technology or disconnecting completely from modern life. The goal is balance.

Modern environments will continue competing for attention constantly. But when people intentionally create moments of stillness, recovery, and conscious attention within those environments, the nervous system gradually becomes less reactive and more internally stable over time.

This is important because clarity rarely develops inside continuous mental noise.

It develops when attention is given enough space to settle.

And in a distracted world, intentionally protecting that space becomes one of the most important forms of emotional and psychological self-care.

Key Insights

- Continuous stimulation reduces psychological space and internal awareness.
- Constant engagement often hides deeper stress, exhaustion, and emotional tension.
- Creating intentional space helps the nervous system recover balance and clarity.
- Stillness may initially feel uncomfortable because the mind has adapted to constant stimulation.
- Awareness becomes stronger when attention has space to slow down and observe clearly.

CHAPTER 8

LIVING WITH AWARENESS IN A DISTRACTED WORLD

SECTION 1: AWARENESS IN EVERYDAY LIFE

Awareness is often misunderstood as something that exists only during quiet reflection, meditation, or moments of deep self-observation.

But real awareness is built during ordinary daily life.

It develops in small moments that most people normally move through automatically:

- noticing stress before reacting impulsively,
- recognizing distraction while it is happening,
- becoming aware of emotional tension before it fully takes control,
- observing attention shifting unconsciously toward stimulation,
- or realizing when the mind is operating from exhaustion instead of clarity.

These moments may appear simple.

But over time, they change the way people experience themselves.

Many individuals spend large parts of life functioning automatically. They wake up mentally occupied, move through responsibilities reactively, consume stimulation continuously, and carry stress throughout the day without fully noticing how deeply those patterns influence attention, emotion, behavior, and overall well-being.

Awareness interrupts that automatic movement.

The more consciously you observe your internal state throughout everyday experiences, the easier it becomes to recognize when:

- the nervous system is overloaded,
- attention is becoming fragmented,
- emotional pressure is increasing,
- or behavior is being driven more by impulse than intention.

This does not require perfect control.

Awareness is not about becoming calm every moment or eliminating every distraction, emotion, or stressful experience from life. It is about noticing what is happening internally with greater honesty and clarity instead of remaining completely unconscious inside repeated patterns.

Over time, this changes daily life in subtle but important ways.

You begin responding more slowly instead of reacting immediately.

You recognize stress earlier before it builds too deeply.

You become more intentional with attention.

You notice when stimulation is replacing recovery.

You become aware of emotional exhaustion before it turns into complete burnout.

These shifts often begin quietly.

A pause before reacting emotionally.

Choosing presence during a conversation.

Noticing the urge to escape discomfort without immediately acting on it.

Allowing moments of stillness without automatically reaching for distraction.

Small moments of awareness repeated consistently gradually reshape the nervous system.

This process is especially important in modern environments because life now moves fast enough that unconscious living can easily become the default state. People remain busy constantly while losing awareness of their own mental and emotional condition underneath the activity.

As a result, many individuals know how to manage responsibilities more effectively than they know how to understand themselves.

Awareness changes that relationship.

You begin living with greater connection to your internal experience instead of remaining continuously pulled outward by stimulation, urgency, pressure, and automatic behavior. Attention becomes more grounded. Emotional reactions become easier to recognize. Presence becomes more accessible even during ordinary moments of life.

And slowly, awareness stops feeling like a practice you occasionally remember.

It becomes a way of moving through life more consciously.

This is where deeper balance begins developing.

Not through perfection.

Not through controlling every thought or emotion.

But through repeatedly returning attention back to the present moment with enough honesty to recognize what is actually happening inside you while life is unfolding.

Because awareness is not something separate from daily life.

It is the way you experience daily life more clearly.

Key Insights

- Awareness is developed through ordinary daily moments, not only during reflection.
- Small moments of conscious observation gradually change behavior and emotional regulation.
- Modern life makes unconscious living feel normal through constant stimulation and busyness.
- Awareness helps recognize stress, exhaustion, and reactivity before they intensify deeply.
- Lasting balance develops through repeatedly returning attention to the present moment.

SECTION 2: BUILDING SUSTAINABLE MENTAL HABITS

Many people approach change with intensity.

They create strict routines, make ambitious promises to themselves, remove distractions aggressively, and try to transform their behavior all at once. For a short period, motivation often feels strong. Attention improves. Productivity increases. The feeling of control returns temporarily.

But extreme change is rarely sustainable for long.

Eventually, stress increases, life becomes busy again, emotional fatigue returns, or motivation weakens — and many people slowly fall back into older patterns. This often creates frustration and self-criticism because they assume lasting change should happen quickly if they simply try hard enough.

But real behavioral change usually develops differently.

Sustainable habits are built through consistency, not intensity.

The nervous system changes gradually through repeated experiences, repeated awareness, and repeated behavioral patterns practiced over time. Small shifts maintained consistently often create deeper long-term transformation than dramatic short-term efforts that become impossible to sustain realistically.

This is important because many people unconsciously approach self-improvement through pressure instead of balance.

They attempt to force change aggressively while already emotionally exhausted, mentally overstimulated, or chronically stressed. As a result, the process itself becomes another source of internal pressure rather than genuine healing or growth.

Sustainable mental habits develop more effectively when awareness guides behavior instead of guilt.

This changes the approach completely.

Instead of asking: "How do I control myself perfectly?"

You begin asking: "What patterns are repeatedly moving me away from balance?"

That shift creates greater honesty and less internal conflict.

Over time, sustainable habits often begin through very small but meaningful adjustments:

- reducing unnecessary stimulation gradually,
- creating more intentional recovery,
- protecting attention more consciously,
- slowing reactive behaviors,
- improving sleep consistency,
- allowing more presence during daily experiences,
- and becoming more aware of emotional triggers before reacting automatically.

These changes may appear simple externally.

But internally, they slowly reshape the nervous system.

One of the most important parts of sustainable change is learning to stop expecting perfection from yourself constantly.

Some days attention will still feel scattered.

Stress will still affect behavior.

Old impulses will still appear.

Distraction will still happen.

Awareness is not about never struggling again.

It is about recognizing patterns more quickly and returning to balance more intentionally instead of remaining trapped inside unconscious cycles for long periods of time.

This process becomes easier when habits support the nervous system instead of overstimulating it continuously.

- Regular recovery.
- Intentional boundaries.
- Focused attention.
- Moments of stillness.
- Reduced emotional overload.
- More conscious engagement with technology and environment.

These experiences gradually strengthen internal stability over time. Sustainable habits also change emotional experience.

- The mind feels less chaotic.
- Presence becomes easier.
- Attention becomes steadier.
- Recovery feels deeper.
- Emotional reactions become less automatic.
- Life begins feeling less driven by urgency and more guided by intentional awareness.

This does not happen through one dramatic breakthrough.

It develops through small repeated choices practiced consistently enough that they slowly become part of the way you live.

Because lasting transformation is rarely built through force. It is built through awareness repeated consistently over time.

Key Insights

- Sustainable habits are built through consistency, not intensity.
- Lasting change develops gradually through repeated awareness and small behavioral shifts.
- Extreme self-control often creates additional pressure instead of balance.
- Awareness helps people return to stability without harsh self-judgment.
- Small intentional habits gradually reshape attention, emotional regulation, and mental clarity.

SECTION 3: THE DAILY CONTROL FRAMEWORK

Modern life continuously pulls attention outward.

Responsibilities, stimulation, urgency, emotional pressure, information, and constant engagement compete for mental space throughout the day. Without some form of intentional structure, many people gradually begin living reactively — responding to whatever feels most urgent, stimulating, or emotionally demanding in the moment.

This is why daily awareness needs practical support.

Not rigid control.

Not extreme discipline.

But simple structures that help the mind remain more balanced, intentional, and internally stable within environments designed to create continuous distraction and overstimulation.

The Daily Control Framework is built around one central idea:small consistent behaviors influence the nervous system more deeply than occasional intense efforts.

Many people wait for motivation before taking care of their attention, emotional state, recovery, or mental clarity. But sustainable balance rarely comes from temporary emotional highs. It develops through repeated daily patterns that gradually shape how the mind and nervous system function over time.

This framework is not about perfection.

It is about creating enough intentional structure to reduce unconscious living.

The first part of the framework is protecting attention intentionally.

This means becoming more aware of what repeatedly consumes mental energy throughout the day.

Not every notification requires immediate response.

Not every moment ofboredom requires stimulation.

Not every emotional discomfort requires distraction or escape.

Attention becomes more stable when it is not continuously fragmented.

The second part is creating moments of recovery deliberately.

Modern life rarely creates recovery automatically anymore. Many people move from one form of stimulation to another without allowing the nervous system enough stillness to reset deeply. Small moments of quiet, slower pacing, intentional rest, and reduced mental input gradually help the mind recover balance again.

The third part is observing emotional patterns honestly.

Stress, exhaustion, frustration, loneliness, boredom, pressure, and emotional overload often influence behavior far more than people realize. The more clearly these internal states are recognized, the easier it becomes to respond consciously instead of reacting automatically.

The fourth part is reducing unnecessary overstimulation consistently.

This does not require abandoning technology or disconnecting from modern life completely. It means becoming more intentional about:

- what consumes attention,
- what increases emotional exhaustion,
- what repeatedly drains mental clarity,

- and what genuinely supports recovery and presence.

Small boundaries create significant long-term effects.

The final part is returning to awareness repeatedly throughout the day.

Noticing when the mind becomes reactive.

Recognizing when stress is shaping behavior.

Observing when attention is being pulled automatically.

Pausing briefly before impulsive reactions.

These moments slowly strengthen conscious attention over time.

What makes this framework sustainable is its simplicity.

Many people fail to maintain change because they try to transform their lives through extreme control. But the nervous system responds more effectively to steady regulation than constant pressure.

- Small repeated actions gradually become patterns.
- Patterns shape emotional regulation.
- Emotional regulation influences attention.
- Attention influences behavior.

- And behavior slowly shapes the quality of daily life itself.

This is why meaningful change often appears quietly before it appears dramatically.

- You become slightly less reactive.
- More present during conversations.
- Less dependent on constant stimulation.
- More aware of emotional exhaustion earlier.
- More intentional with attention and energy.

Over time, these shifts create something many people are searching for without fully realizing it: a mind that feels calmer, clearer, and less controlled by automatic patterns.

Not because life becomes perfect externally.

But because awareness begins guiding the way you move through it internally.

Key Insights

- Small daily patterns influence the nervous system more deeply than intense short-term efforts.
- Protecting attention and creating recovery intentionally are essential in modern life.
- Awareness helps reduce reactive and unconscious living gradually over time.

- Sustainable balance develops through consistent regulation, not extreme control.
- Lasting change often begins through small repeated moments of intentional awareness.

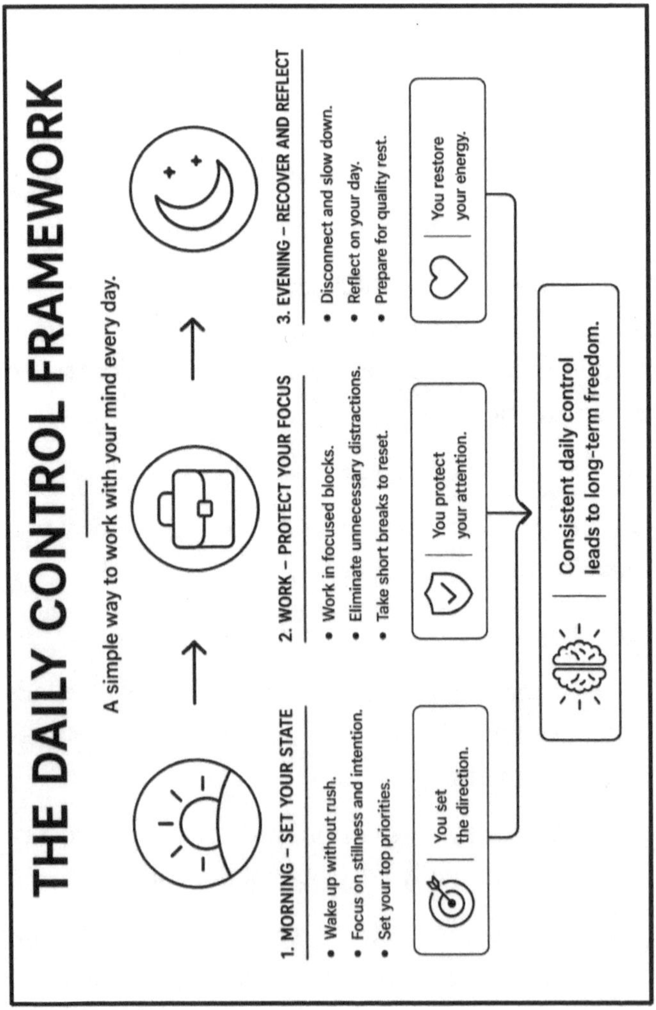

SECTION 4: LONG-TERM CHANGE THROUGH SMALL SHIFTS

Many people believe transformation happens through dramatic moments.

A sudden breakthrough.

A perfect routine.

Complete discipline.

A major life decision that changes everything instantly.

But lasting internal change usually develops much more quietly.

The nervous system changes gradually through repeated experiences, repeated awareness, and repeated behavioral patterns practiced consistently over time. Small shifts that appear insignificant in the moment often create the deepest long-term effects because they slowly reshape how attention, emotion, and behavior operate every day.

This is why sustainable growth rarely feels dramatic while it is happening.

At first, the changes may seem almost invisible.

You pause slightly more before reacting emotionally.

You notice stress earlier.

You become more aware of when attention is drifting automatically.

You recover more intentionally after mentally exhausting days.

You spend less time unconsciously escaping discomfort through stimulation.

These shifts may appear small externally.

But internally, they represent important changes in awareness and nervous system regulation.

Over time, repeated small adjustments begin influencing larger parts of life.

- Attention becomes steadier.
- Mental clarity improves gradually.
- Emotional reactions become less impulsive.
- Stillness feels less uncomfortable.
- Relationships become more present.
- Recovery becomes deeper.

- The mind feels less controlled by constant urgency, stimulation, and reactivity.

This process is important to understand because many people unknowingly sabotage progress by expecting immediate perfection.

- They assume change is failing if old habits still appear occasionally.
- If distraction still happens.
- If stress still affects attention.
- If emotional exhaustion sometimes returns.

But real change is rarely linear.

There will still be difficult days.

The mind will still become reactive sometimes.

Old patterns may still return under pressure.

Awareness does not eliminate being human.

It changes how quickly you recognize when you are moving away from balance and how intentionally you return to it afterward.

That difference matters deeply.

A person living unconsciously inside stress, stimulation, and emotional reactivity may remain trapped in unhealthy cycles for years without fully recognizing what is happening internally.

But a person developing awareness begins noticing patterns earlier.

Recovery begins sooner.

Reactions become less automatic.

The nervous system gradually spends less time trapped in continuous overload.

Small awareness consistently changes direction over time.

This is why long-term transformation is often built through ordinary moments rather than extraordinary ones:

- protecting attention slightly more consciously,
- creating small periods of stillness,
- reducing unnecessary stimulation,
- recognizing emotional exhaustion earlier,
- responding with greater awareness instead of immediate reaction,
- and repeatedly returning attention back to the present moment.

These moments slowly accumulate.

And eventually, the internal experience of life begins changing.

The mind feels less chaotic.

Presence becomes easier.

Emotional balance becomes more accessible.

Life no longer feels driven entirely by automatic impulses, constant pressure, or endless mental movement.

This does not create a perfect life free from stress or difficulty.

But it creates something more sustainable:

the ability to live with greater awareness, steadiness, and intentionality inside a world that constantly pulls attention away from itself.

And in many ways, that quiet shift is where real transformation begins.

Key Insights

- Lasting change develops gradually through repeated small shifts over time.
- Sustainable growth often feels subtle while it is happening.
- Awareness helps people return to balance more intentionally after stress or reactivity.
- Small daily choices gradually reshape attention, emotional regulation, and mental clarity.
- Real transformation is built through consistency and awareness, not perfection.

CONCLUSION

RETURNING TO YOURSELF

Modern life moves fast.

Attention is constantly pulled outward toward information, stimulation, urgency, pressure, achievement, distraction, and endless engagement. Over time, many people become so accustomed to this constant movement that they stop noticing how deeply it affects their mind, nervous system, emotions, and overall sense of inner stability.

The result is not always dramatic.

Sometimes it appears quietly.

A restless mind that struggles to slow down.

Emotional exhaustion hidden beneath productivity.

The inability to stay present for long.

A constant search for stimulation without fully understanding why.

Feeling mentally occupied even during moments that are supposed to feel restful.

For a long time, I did not fully understand these patterns in my own life either.

Like many people, I believed the solution was simply more discipline, better control, stronger routines, or greater productivity. But over time, I slowly realized something deeper: many of the struggles I was experiencing were not only about motivation or willpower.

They were connected to the way modern life continuously shaped attention, emotion, stress, and behavior beneath conscious awareness.

The more I began observing these patterns honestly, the more clearly I understood how easily people can become disconnected from themselves while still appearing functional externally.

This book was never written to promote perfection.

It was written to create awareness.

Because awareness changes the relationship you have with your mind.

The moment you begin recognizing your internal patterns more clearly, something important shifts. Stress becomes easier to notice before it completely overwhelms you. Attention becomes more intentional. Emotional reactions become less automatic. Recovery becomes more meaningful. Life begins feeling less driven by unconscious impulses and more guided by conscious presence.

Not perfectly.

But gradually.

This is important to remember because real transformation rarely happens through one dramatic breakthrough. Most lasting change develops quietly through repeated small moments of awareness:

- noticing distraction,
- recognizing emotional exhaustion,
- slowing reactive behavior,
- creating space for stillness,
- protecting attention more intentionally,
- and returning to the present moment again and again.

These moments may seem small.

But over time, they change the way you experience life internally.

- You begin feeling calmer.
- More aware.
- Less mentally scattered.

- Less controlled by constant urgency.
- More capable of being fully present with yourself, your work, your relationships, and your daily experiences.

The goal is not to escape modern life completely.

The goal is to move through it more consciously.

Because the world will continue competing for your attention every day. Stimulation will continue increasing. Pressure will continue existing. Distraction will remain easily available.

But awareness gives you something powerful within all of it:

the ability to pause,

to notice,

and to choose intentionally instead of reacting automatically.

That space changes everything.

Over time, you begin understanding that real freedom is not found through constant stimulation, endless productivity, or perfect control over life.

Real freedom begins when you are no longer completely controlled by unconscious patterns within yourself.

And perhaps that is what returning to yourself truly means.

Not becoming someone entirely different.

But slowly reconnecting with the clarity, balance, presence, and awareness that were buried beneath the noise for too long.

Thank you for taking this journey with me.

I hope this book helps you move through life with greater awareness, deeper balance, and a calmer relationship with your own mind.

One moment of awareness at a time.

FINAL REFLECTIONS

Dopamine is not the pursuit of pleasure. It is the anticipation of possibility.

Cortisol is not the enemy. It is a system designed to prepare you for pressure and uncertainty.

Many modern behaviors are not random habits, but repeated responses to internal discomfort and external stimulation.

The more fragmented attention becomes, the more mentally unsettled life begins to feel.

Temporary relief is not always true recovery. Some distractions only delay deeper awareness.

Awareness begins the moment you notice a pattern while it is happening.

A pause between impulse and action creates space for conscious choice.

Modern environments are designed to compete continuously for your attention and emotional energy.

Rest is not simply the absence of activity. It is the ability of the nervous system to fully settle.

Lasting change develops through repeated moments of awareness, not force alone.

You do not need to eliminate desire or stress. You need to understand your relationship with them.

The goal is not perfect control, but conscious participation in how you respond to life.

The more clearly you recognize your patterns, the less automatically they begin controlling you.

Small shifts repeated consistently gradually reshape attention, emotion, and behavior over time.

Awareness does not remove life's pressures, but it changes how deeply they control your inner world.

ABOUT THE AUTHOR

Subrata Kumar Patel is a seasoned Human Resources professional with nearly two decades of experience working closely with people, workplaces, performance systems, and organizational behavior. Over the years, his work has gone beyond processes and professional structures into something deeper — understanding the emotional and psychological realities people quietly carry beneath modern life and work.

Through years of observing burnout, stress, attention fragmentation, emotional fatigue, and the growing pressure of constant responsiveness, he became increasingly interested in how modern environments shape human behavior, focus, and emotional well-being.

His interest in human psychology, awareness, and behavioral patterns eventually led him toward exploring the relationship between dopamine, cortisol, attention, and modern living — not from a purely scientific perspective, but from a deeply human one.

This book reflects that journey of observation, reflection, and understanding.

Rather than offering extreme solutions or motivational shortcuts, Subrata believes lasting change begins with awareness — the ability to recognize how modern life continuously influences the way people think, feel, react, and experience themselves internally.

Through his writing, he hopes to help readers better understand their own patterns, reconnect with greater clarity and balance, and move through life with more conscious awareness in an increasingly distracted world.

www.ingramcontent.com/pod-product-compliance
Lightning Source LLC
LaVergne TN
LVHW100314210926
848480LV00003B/1114

* 9 7 9 8 9 0 5 6 0 3 5 5 6 *